Vocation and Violence

As #MeToo and its sister movement #ChurchToo demonstrated, sexual violence is systemic in many and varied workplace settings, including Christian churches, and can destroy women's careers and vocational aspirations.

The study draws on empirical evidence – personal stories from survivors and the views of church leaders and educators – in dialogue with theoretical perspectives, to consider clergy sexual abuse of adult women and the conditions that support it. Institutional abuse only changes when survivors come forward. This study focusses on New Zealand Anglicanism, the locus of the author's experience, and has resonance for a range of denominational settings. It aims to be a useful resource to clergy, ministry educators, and those training for ministry, and to academics and scholars with an interest in theology, gender, and professional ethics. Notably, it will be a potentially helpful text for women survivors of sexual misconduct by clergy, not least those who are considering a future in the church or grieving the loss of one.

The volume concludes by suggesting that alternative theological models and relational ethics are essential if the church is to truly address the problem of clergy sexual abuse and give greater priority to the abused.

Miryam Clough is a Postdoctoral Fellow at The College of St John the Evangelist/Hoani Tapu te Kaikauwhau i te Rongopai, Auckland, New Zealand.

T0371794

Rape Culture, Religion and the Bible

Series Editors:
Caroline Blyth, *University of Auckland, New Zealand*
Johanna Stiebert, *University of Leeds, UK*

Rape Myths, the Bible and #MeToo
Johanna Stiebert

Telling Terror in Judges 19
Rape and Reparation for the Levite's wife
Helen Paynter

Resisting Rape Culture
The Hebrew Bible and Hong Kong Sex Workers
Nany Nan Hoon Tan

The Bible and Sexual Violence against Men
Chris Greenough

Rape Culture, Purity Culture, and Coercive Control in Teen Girl Bibles
Caroline Blyth

Trafficking Hadassah
Collective Trauma, Cultural Memory, and Identity in the Book of Esther and in the African Diaspora
Ericka Shawndricka Dunbar

Vocation and Violence
The Church and #MeToo
Miryam Clough

For more information about this series, please visit: https://www.routledge.com/Rape-Culture-Religion-and-the-Bible/book-series/RCRB

Vocation and Violence
The Church and #MeToo

Miryam Clough

Routledge
Taylor & Francis Group

LONDON AND NEW YORK

First published 2022
by Routledge
4 Park Square, Milton Park, Abingdon, Oxon OX14 4RN

and by Routledge
605 Third Avenue, New York, NY 10158

Routledge is an imprint of the Taylor & Francis Group, an informa business

British Library Cataloguing-in-Publication Data
A catalogue record for this book is available from the British Library

Library of Congress Cataloging-in-Publication Data
A catalog record has been requested for this book

ISBN: 978-0-367-75145-6 (hbk)
ISBN: 978-0-367-75971-1 (pbk)
ISBN: 978-1-003-16493-7 (ebk)

DOI: 10.4324/9781003164937

Typeset in Times New Roman
by codeMantra

Contents

Acknowledgements

I did not set out to write a book on clergy sexual misconduct; the topic emerged in the course of a wider research project on women in the church. In writing it, I have been conscious of my own vulnerability in telling a story that has been painful and shaming over many years. The courage and tenacity of other survivors of clergy abuse have inspired and encouraged me in this project, and I am grateful to all those who have shared their personal stories with me. In particular, I acknowledge those, survivors and others, whose stories and perspectives are shared in these pages and who continue to call the church to account: Revd Louise Deans, Trish McBride, 'Jane', Archbishop Philip Richardson, Dr Rocío Figueroa, 'Sarah', Dr Emily Colgan, Dr Paul Reynolds, Jacinda Thompson, and those who are not named.

I am grateful to Revd Canon Tony Gerritsen, Revd Katene Eruera, and the St John's College Trust Board for two periods at the college as a visiting scholar, and to the college community and the staff at the John Kinder Theological Library, who have been so supportive of my work.

I am especially grateful to Jess, Annie, and Mike who have let me move to the other side of the world to pursue my vocation, and to Bishop Te Kitohi Pikaahu for his sensitive, thoughtful, and creative response to my experience of the church.

Finally, I would like to thank Professor David Tombs and Dr Tess Patterson for their support with my research, my sister Dr Robyn Clough, for her insightful comments on the manuscript, and Professor Johanna Stiebert and Dr Caroline Blyth, for their editorial support and encouragement throughout the process.

1 Introduction

#MeToo, #ChurchToo

This volume will demonstrate that #MeToo is as relevant within the church as in the secular arena and that clergy, who are often held in the public imagination to be 'above' abusive or criminal activity, are as susceptible to personal and professional boundary violations as those in secular positions of power. Specifically, it will draw attention to a hitherto neglected aspect of clergy sexual misconduct: its effects on the vocations of women in the church. Additionally, it will examine some of the discourses within the Christian tradition that produce rape culture: the culture in which the sexual abuse and exploitation of women by men is facilitated and sustained.

In 2006, African American civil rights activist Tarana Burke founded *me too*, a movement instigated to provide support and advocacy for women and girls of colour from low-income communities who had suffered sexual abuse, and to interrupt sexual violence.[1] As a youth worker, Burke had regretted not disclosing her own experience of abuse to a young girl who had confided that her stepfather was sexually abusing her. Burke recognised that the simple phrase 'me too' would have reduced the girl's sense of isolation and shame and enabled her to seek support.

In October 2017, in response to reports of multiple accusations of sexual abuse against Hollywood film producer Harvey Weinstein, actor Alyssa Milano encouraged women who had been abused to respond to her on Twitter with the statement 'me too' to foreground the scale and magnitude of sexual abuse. Overnight, Milano's tweet went viral. As #MeToo rapidly gained momentum, countless women in the film industry, politics, the media, and academia revealed that they too had similar experiences.

DOI: 10.4324/9781003164937-1

Social media quickly took this expanding narrative of sexual abuse further, beyond the workplace into homes, schools, university and college campuses, churches, mosques, synagogues, and temples, into hospitals and clinics, political and social gatherings, into social care organisations and communities. Many men were shocked by the scale of it. Perhaps few women were surprised. #MeToo confirmed that sexual abuse is pandemic in scope, and its incidence is overwhelming.

In November 2017, #MeToo was joined by #ChurchToo, the hashtag coined by American former evangelicals Emily Joy and Hannah Pasch, whose revelations of abuse by church leaders triggered a flood of similar disclosures from women and men in predominantly evangelical churches around the world. In 2018, journalist Becca Andrews commented, '[a] reckoning has been a long time coming for the evangelical community'. Prior to this, periodic disclosures of abuse by leaders in America's evangelical megachurches had attracted significant media attention, prompting critical discussion of the patriarchal theology espoused by the churches' predominantly white, heterosexual male pastors. However, most of these cases had soon faded from view with only minimal repercussions for the men involved (Andrews 2018). Subsequent to #ChurchToo, formal accusations of abuse by church leaders skyrocketed. By July 2019, over 100 Southern Baptist pastors and a number of leaders of evangelical megachurches across America were the subjects of abuse complaints (Barnett 2019).

The Weinstein scandal alone had demonstrated that dozens of young women with serious and passionate aspirations in the film industry – hard-working, talented young women who were earnestly pursuing their vocations – had found themselves subjected to sexual harassment and abuse. Instead of being supported and mentored by senior men in their field in the way their young male colleagues would be, these women were coerced or forced into unwanted sexual activity, often silenced by the promise of work if they complied and the very real threat of failure if they did not. How did Weinstein get away with abusing so many women and for so many years?

Despite nearly half a century of sexual harassment legislation, this abusive culture has clearly been slow to change. A poll conducted by MSN in 2017 showed that 45% of women respondents reported experiencing sexual harassment at work and that three times as many women as men reported experiencing workplace sexual harassment. Seventy-three percent of women and 81% of men had never reported their abuse (Gillett 2017).

#ChurchToo has highlighted that sexual harassment and abuse is no less prevalent in Christian communities and workplaces than in secular ones. While many churches began developing policies to address clergy misconduct in the 1990s, understanding of this issue remains limited. Victims may be blamed for the abuse they experience and shunned by their local churches. Equally, they may be re-victimised and silenced by unwieldy and intrusive processes driven by lawyers and insurers. A high level of cognitive dissonance may occur when respected church leaders are accused of abuse. In early 2020, for example, an internal investigation conducted by L'Arche International established that its esteemed Catholic founder, Jean Vanier, had engaged in coercive sexual relationships with at least six women to whom he had been offering spiritual guidance. The revelations caused widespread dismay (L'Arche International 2020). The reluctance to accept that church leaders are capable of abuse means that victims are often not believed. However, data from a range of sources suggests that false allegations of sexual abuse are unusual and that genuine cases are vastly under-reported (Berglund 2020, 61). The process of reporting abuse is often so traumatic and costly that victims are too afraid to do it.

Effect on vocations

One aspect of clergy sexual harassment and abuse that is under-represented in the body of literature on this subject is the impact that this form of gendered violence has on women's careers in the church, indeed on their vocations to Christian ministry. That is the focus of this volume.

What happens to the vocation of a young woman when the boss who coerces her into a sexual relationship is a priest or minister? Where does responsibility lie in this scenario and how do the church hierarchy and wider Christian community manage the situation when it comes to light? What biblical, theological, and wider socio-cultural discourses underpin the way such situations are perceived and managed? Whose vocation is respected and validated and whose is refuted and denied? To brutally obstruct an individual's vocation through sexual misconduct is to violate not only their emotional and physical boundaries, but their sense of purpose, their spiritual integrity, and their personhood.

While I have found accounts in the literature of or by women who were variously lay church leaders, seminarians, clergy, or nuns, detailing their abuse and the way their lives and ministry were affected by it, there is not, to my knowledge, a discrete text that focusses in any depth on the effects of clergy misconduct on women's vocations. This volume is an attempt to bridge that gap and to foreground the specific injustice dealt to those women whose ministry has been undermined or whose vocations have been denied because a clergyman failed to maintain his professional boundaries.

In more conservative churches where discourses of male headship and female subordination dominate, male sexual prowess and aggressiveness are tolerated, if not actively encouraged, while female worth is tied to sexual purity and restraint. Women are essentially second-class citizens. Even in more liberal churches, the legacy of the patriarchal Christian tradition leaves its traces. In such an environment, it follows that any woman who has a vocation to church leadership may have to fight for it. If she has been forced or coerced into sexual activity with a male cleric, that struggle will be all the more difficult. At the very least, clergy harassment or abuse will constitute a profound distraction from her spiritual path. Most likely, it will impede or end the progress of her vocation and ministry. A vocation is more than just a job. It touches a person's very identity and their relationship with God, the essence of who they are. When it is violated, the wounds run deep and long.

To harm the vocation of another is a fundamental violence. To obstruct God's calling of an individual to ministry on the basis of gender is a profound arrogance. That arrogance is also evident when churches and individuals within them obstruct the vocations of others on the basis of race, colour, disability, or sexual orientation. Jesus did not set out to create a cult of middle class, straight, white men, but if we look at the hierarchies of the main Christian denominations in the West, that is often what we see.

Conversely, many of Jesus' first witnesses were women: old women, bleeding women, foreign women, 'fallen' women. God chose a young unmarried woman to be the mother of Jesus, yet churches grossly abused young unmarried mothers for decades by incarcerating them in punitive mother and baby homes and Magdalen laundries and taking their babies.[2] God has chosen countless women to minister in the church, but men have said 'no', and men have said 'stay silent'. More than this, some men have chosen to exploit the vocations of some of those women for their own sexual gratification.

Terminology and scope of the study

Clergy sexual misconduct occurs in all Christian denominations and for ease, unless I am making a specific point about a particular denomination, I will use the term 'the church' as an umbrella designation for Western institutional Christianity.

Some survivors of clergy sexual misconduct prefer to describe their experience as abuse. I have struggled to describe my personal experience as abuse, preferring the term 'misconduct', although some may feel this term does not give sufficient weight to the issue. Perhaps this is a defence on my part. It is never easy to acknowledge that one has been the victim of abuse or to fully recognise the long-term effects of it (Stephenson 2016, 13). I use the terms 'sexual misconduct' and 'sexual abuse' interchangeably and use the term 'sexual harassment' to describe unwanted, non-physical violations (e.g., sexual innuendo, unwelcome comments, persistent unwanted attention). In each case, I am describing or referring to the violation of a personal and professional boundary by a member of the clergy or church leadership who is in a position of power by virtue of his role in relation to a congregant, student, or counselee. Such violations vary in nature and degree from case to case. They may involve verbal harassment or abuse, emotional and/or spiritual manipulation. They may involve sexual activity that appears to be consensual but is not because of the power imbalance in the relationship, or they may involve physical intrusion and violence. What these violations have in common is that they are located in the areas of sexuality and gender, and they involve the abuse of power, trust, and fiduciary duty.[3]

Any sexually intrusive act is an act of violence. This includes acts of sexual harassment that are often thought to be less serious – abusive comments, wolf-whistling, and sexual innuendo, for instance. These are, in fact, foundational elements in a misogynist culture that produces more egregious acts of sexual and gender-based violence that start with uninvited touch and groping and end with rape and murder. The trivialising of any form of sexual harassment, assault, or misconduct and the failure to name it as such – misnaming a breach of fiduciary duty as 'an affair', for instance – serves only to perpetuate the oppression that is gender-based violence.

While it is the case that both men and women abuse and both men and women are victims of abuse, there is a consensus among professionals and researchers in the field that most clergy abusers are men and most adult victims are women (Cooper-White 2013, 62; Garland 2013, 121). This text will focus mainly, but not exclusively, on the abuse of adult women by male clergy and will refer to abusers as male and to victims as female. All abuse is unacceptable, unprofessional, unethical, and can have devastating consequences irrespective of the genders of the perpetrator and the victim. There is not scope in this volume for a wider exploration of clergy misconduct. This has been, and no doubt will continue to be taken up elsewhere. To provide context however, I will touch briefly here on clergy abuse of children and young people.

Child sexual abuse by clergy

In 2003, the *Boston Globe* won a Pulitzer Prize for public service for exposing systemic child sexual abuse by Catholic clergy in the Boston area. In the 20 or so years prior to that, sporadic revelations of clergy abuse were viewed as isolated incidents, and the subject was not widely discussed (Henley 2010). In 2018, more than 300 priests in Pennsylvania were found to have sexually abused over 1000 children since 1947 (Clohessy 2018), while in Australia, the Royal Commission into Institutional Responses to Child Sexual Abuse received over 4000 reports of sexual abuse of children in religious institutions. Perpetrators included clergy, religious brothers and sisters, church elders, teachers, care workers, and youth group leaders (Commonwealth of Australia 2017, 11). The report notes that while such abuse is by no means unique to the church, there were more allegations of abuse in religious institutions than in those run by any other management group. Church-based abuse is, the report states, particularly disturbing due to the high level of trust and respect placed in that institution, and the consequences for victims and their families are devastating, with lasting impacts on faith and belief. In the main, the perpetrators of abuse in religious institutions were 'people that children and parents trusted the most and suspected the least' (ibid. 12). Case studies conducted by the inquiry revealed that church leaders knew of abuse and either failed to act or acted to protect perpetrators. Notably, '[i]nstitutional reputations and individual perpetrators were prioritised over the needs of victims and their families' (ibid. 11). The cost of confronting abuse is high. Anglican Bishop of Newcastle and clergy abuse survivor Greg Thompson resigned in 2017 after his attempts to expose clergy abuse led to a sustained campaign against him by church members (Davey 2017). Thompson described efforts to conceal extensive child abuse by clergy in the diocese as a 'religious protection racket' (Wakatama 2017).

At the time of writing, inquiries into abuse in care are underway in the UK and in New Zealand. In both the Australian and UK inquiries, misogyny, clericalism, and a failure to be open and non-shaming about sexuality have been identified as contributing factors to child abuse within the church.[4] According to the Independent Inquiry into Child Sexual Abuse's (IICSA)'s report on the Anglican Church in the UK (2020, vi)

> [t]he culture of the Church of England facilitated it becoming a place where abusers could hide. Deference to the authority of the Church and to individual priests, taboos surrounding discussion

of sexuality and an environment where alleged perpetrators were treated more supportively than victims presented barriers to disclosure that many victims could not overcome. Another aspect of the Church's culture was clericalism, which meant that the moral authority of clergy was widely perceived as beyond reproach.

In October 2020, IICSA (2020, 5–6) revealed that 390 Anglican clergy have been charged for sexual offences against children since the 1940s, with an additional 330 civil claims against the Church of England for sexual offending mostly occurring prior to 1990. The report 'criticised the entire moral purpose of the Anglican Church', suggesting it had prioritised its reputation over the well-being of children (BBC Radio 4, 2020). Like the Australian report, the UK report recognises that the extent of offending cannot be known. A key recommendation of the report (IICSA 2020, vi) is that bishops are removed from any safeguarding jurisdiction. Gilo, a campaigner and survivor of clergy abuse, commented on the BBC's *PM* programme (BBC Radio 4, 2020) that this recommendation demonstrates a complete lack of trust in the church leadership and its dysfunctional structure.

In 2018, Aotearoa[5] New Zealand initiated a Royal Commission into Abuse in Care with a remit to investigate abuse of children and vulnerable adults in state care between 1950 and 1999, and discretion to consider cases occurring both before and after that period. The timeframe was subsequently extended to 2019. Settings include social welfare, education, and health and disability care. Subsequently, the terms of reference were extended to include faith-based institutions. The Anglican Church was among the groups which had advocated for this extension. An interim report dated 29 September 2020 placed the financial cost of state and faith-based institutional abuse of children and vulnerable adults as up to $217 billion, with an estimated cost to individuals of $857,000 (MartinJenkins 2020a).[6]

As of July 2020, 1,332 survivors had registered. Of these around 26% experienced abuse in faith-based care settings, broadly consistent with the Commission's estimate that 30% of survivors will be in the faith-based care cohort (MartinJenkins 2020b, 4). Survivor evidence from this cohort was presented to the Commission in 2020 and the faith-based institution redress hearings took place in March 2021. The nature of abuse covered by the Commission includes sexual, physical, and psychological abuse, neglect, and bullying, including 'inadequate or improper treatment or care that resulted in serious harm to the individual (whether mental or physical)' (Abuse in Care 2018, 8:17.1). Much of the abuse presented to the Commission, including that pertaining to faith-based institutions, occurred in children's homes and schools. Abuse in an Anglican mother and baby home, St Mary's Home for Unwed Mothers, also featured. Other contexts for abuse of adults include disabled care settings, psychiatric institutions, and law enforcement settings.

Abuse of adult women

In its focus on children and vulnerable adults in care, the Commission's relevance to this volume is in some respects limited. However, evidence of the Anglican Church's response to disclosures of abuse historically, and the way this response is evolving due to its participation in the Commission is directly relevant and is discussed in this volume, primarily in Chapter 4. Additionally, at least two Anglican women have submitted evidence to the Commission on the basis that, although they were adults when abuse by clergy occurred, they were vulnerable at that time due to the relative power differential in those relationships, in which the offenders had a duty of care and professional responsibility. The circumstances contributing to this type of vulnerability are discussed in Chapter 2.

American Presbyterian minister and clergy abuse survivor, Ruth Everhart (2020, 13) notes that, '[t]o open our eyes to the lived experience of women is to open our eyes to abuse'. While the scale of the child abuse crisis in the church has shocked Christians and non-Christians worldwide, Dr Gerardine Robinson, an expert in the treatment of clergy abusers who gave evidence to the Australian Royal Commission, asserts that the number of women abused by clergy is four times the number of child victims (Tomazin 2018). Union Theological Seminary Professor Pamela Cooper-White, also an expert in the field of clergy sexual abuse, estimates that 90–95% of the victims of clergy sexual exploitation are female congregants (Batchelor 2013, xv) and notes that clergy abuse of adult women is much more prevalent than commonly supposed, with some estimates of the proportion of male clergy who abuse women exceeding the 5–13% figure assigned to male psychotherapists (Cooper-White 2013, 60). These figures are concerning and underline the importance of research in this area.

Former Bishop of Dunedin, Penny Jamieson (1997, 106) notes that this insidious symptom of the church's gendered power dynamics manifested in New Zealand as women moved into ministry roles alongside men. Writing in the US around the same time, Nils Friberg and Mark Laaser (1998, 47) comment that 'the growing number of women who have sought ordination have begun to expose the amount of sexual harassment and abuse that they have suffered at the hands of male professors, supervisors and ecclesiastical superiors'. As women have sought equality with men in ministry, they observe (p. 48), men have worked hard to maintain control of women by 'sexually objectifying and manipulating them'. Arguably, the church's slowness to recognise and deal with systemic clergy misconduct is as indicative of its entrenched resistance to gender equality as it is of its desperation to hold on to its diminishing authority.

Pervasiveness of clergy abuse

Clergy sexual abuse of all kinds has a long history (Doyle, Sipe, and Wall 2006). While no one denomination has a monopoly on it, the extent of revealed abuse in the Catholic Church is illuminating for all faith communities (Sipe 2007, xv) and persists because it is actively enabled by the church's hierarchy, which has been content to maintain power at the expense of its victims and its public record (Clohessy 2018; Kennedy 2019). Clerical self-interest is compounded by the influence of lawyers and insurers.[7] The focus on litigation has hindered attempts to understand and address clergy abuse as a systemic issue. Rather than attempting to reduce the abuse crisis by investing in adequate research, training, and prevention, resources are directed to protecting the church's reputation and silencing victims. In an article about cross-denominational clergy abuse, Dr Doug Weiss, a clinical psychologist in Colorado, makes a similar point. It is not that church members do not want to address the issue of clergy misconduct, it is that church leaders are not willing to make themselves and their peers accountable for their behaviour (Berglund 2020, 60).

In the UK, media reporting on clergy abuse scandals and recent publications such as *Letters to a Broken Church* (Fife and Gilo 2019) and *To Heal and Not to Hurt* (Harper and Wilson 2019) demonstrate that, as in the Catholic Church, the clergy abuse scandal in the Church of England is by no means over and the institutional response to abuse allegations has been far from adequate, with lawyers and insurers contributing to its dysfunction.

Hopefully, in Aotearoa New Zealand the tide is finally turning, largely due to the resilience and persistence of survivors, including Jacinda Thompson. After 15 years attempting to call the Anglican Church to account, Thompson took her case to the Human Rights Review Tribunal, resulting in a $100,000 settlement and an undertaking from the church to improve its vetting, training, and complaints processes (Johnston 2020). Like Thompson, Anglican priest, Louise

Deans, whose story is discussed in Chapter 2, has also courageously persisted in holding the church to account, most recently by giving evidence to the Royal Commission. However, few cases to date have received the public scrutiny that these have, and it is questionable whether cases that remain out of the public eye are dealt with fairly.

The systemic nature of clergy abuse

The exploration of clergy sexual misconduct in this volume is underpinned by the hypothesis that biblical, theological, and social constructs combine to create contexts in which (predominantly) male clergy and church leaders can abuse others and get away with it, while the victims of their unprofessional actions and violence pay a high price on many levels. The masculinist-gendered constructs that have made the church a safe-haven for abusers and a minefield for others, particularly those who are vulnerable, or at vulnerable points in some aspect of their lives, are outlined in subsequent chapters. Throughout this volume I attempt to ground theoretical assertions in empirical data; both to ensure that the text is widely accessible, and to provide evidence of the systemic failings – and their consequences – that many in church leadership would rather sweep under the carpet.

Clergy sexual misconduct does not happen in a vacuum. It emerges as the product of a faulty system: a system that privileges male experience and male desire, that produces male entitlement and that legitimises male violence. It is the product of a system in which masculinist theology both justifies and creates the conditions for unprofessional and abusive behaviour by predominantly male clergy against women, children, and some men. Church-based abuse is a systemic issue, and it requires a systemic approach.

In addressing clergy misconduct, it is necessary to examine the distribution and nature of power in the church; we must ask 'what is the situation and who holds the power in the system'.[8] Equally, in dealing with individual cases, churches are wise not to restrict their response to the two individuals involved, but need to recognise and address abuse by clergy as a very complex situation that has repercussions for many people and for the church's credibility in the world (Hopkins 1993, 1). The claim that an offending priest is employed not by the church in which he works, but by God, thereby relieving the church leadership of vicarious responsibility for his actions, will no longer wash – as indeed Thompson's successful case against the Anglican Church demonstrated (Johnston 2020).[9]

Impact on the wider church

The Wilberforce Foundation's 2018 McCrindle report *Faith and Belief in New Zealand* describes New Zealand as an increasingly secular nation with more than half (55%) of New Zealanders not identifying with any main religion. While one-third of New Zealanders identify as Christian (either Protestant/Evangelical/Pentecostal or Catholic/ Orthodox), only 17% of New Zealanders attend church at least monthly and only 9% are actively involved. While many New Zealanders recognise the benefits of spirituality and one in four values the positive contribution of Christianity to New Zealand society particularly in the area of social justice (p. 40), the report identified a number of obstacles preventing people exploring Christianity further. The key blocker to engagement with Christianity is the church's teaching and stance on homosexuality (47%). Other issues included public perceptions of 'exclusivity and judgement', gender inequality, and poor attitudes to women and unmarried mothers (pp. 40–42). Seventy-six percent cited church abuse as having a negative influence on their perception of the church and as contributing to Christianity's decline in New Zealand, and 69% indicated hypocrisy – Christians not practising what they preach – as having a negative effect. Other negative perceptions concerned money, authoritarianism, exclusivity, and the church being out of date and out of touch (pp. 43–44).

In response to the so-called 'pastoral' guidance on same and opposite sex civil partnerships issued by the Church of England's House of Bishops in December 2019,[10] Jayne Ozanne (Sherwood 2020) makes a similar observation, commenting on the nation's bewilderment at the judgementalism of an institution that purports to promote the love of God. Additionally, she foregrounds the hypocrisy of a church that urges unmarried opposite sex and all same-sex couples to practice sexual abstinence while those among its clergy are guilty of adultery, sexual harassment, and sexual abuse. Clergy get away with this abuse of power, she says, 'because they can' (ibid.).

The effects of clergy sexual misconduct are far-reaching (Batchelor 2013, xv). Abuse affects more than the two individuals at its core. Its effects radiate out to the families of the victim and of her abuser, and to the wider church congregation. If the situation is made public, the betrayal of trust at the centre ripples further, affecting others in the wider church community and influencing the perception those outside the institution have of it.

A rapidly dwindling church cannot afford to ignore public perceptions of its teachings and behaviours. Church leaders are unwise to assume that they can continue to hoodwink the public about sex and gender discrimination and abuse and retain their credibility. Those who do so are doing Christianity and the gospel a profound disservice.

Breaking the silence on clergy sexual misconduct is essential if churches are to effect change and if all women are to be safe at vulnerable times in their lives when they may seek or be offered support from a church leader. Telling the story of abuse may be an important aspect of the healing process for the offended against, or, indeed, an alternative method of seeking justice when the pastoral and/or judicial response of the church has been inadequate. As with #MeToo, public interest tends to lie with the details of the abuse. Certainly, once any legal process is underway obsession with the detail escalates (especially in the hands of the media) as victims are required to substantiate their claims and abusers seek to argue that any sexual activity was consensual. The focus of this volume is not, however, the detail of what happened. Nor is it concerned, as much of the literature to date is, on the effects of clergy abuse on congregations. Rather, its concern is with the effects on women's vocations. This is an aspect that has been only minimally addressed in the literature thus far. How, this volume asks, did clergy abuse affect the vocations of those women who felt called to ministry in the church? What were the spiritual repercussions of this profound violation of professional boundaries for those women and what were the practical consequences?

Methodology

This study utilises autoethnography and narrative to explore the effects of clergy sexual abuse and of sexism on women's vocations to Christian ministry. Autoethnography is a qualitative research method that explores social and cultural contexts through the lens of the self – via an analysis of the personal experience of the researcher – using stories to help people make sense of themselves and others within meaningful and ethical frameworks. Autoethnography challenges the so-called objectivity of conventional research methods, treating research as a political tool for social justice that aims to produce

> meaningful, accessible, and evocative research grounded in personal experience … [and to] sensitize readers to issues of identity politics, *to experiences shrouded in silence*, and to forms of representation that deepen our capacity to empathize with people who are different from us.
> (Ellis, Adams, and Bochner 2011, 1 emphasis mine)

In recognising the legitimacy and authority of personal stories – with their implicit subjectivity and emotionality – autoethnography allows differing truths to unfold, dominant discourses to be challenged and marginalised voices to be heard. 'For the most part', Ellis, Adams, and Bochner (2011, 1) assert, 'those who advocate and insist on canonical forms of doing and writing research are advocating a White, masculine, heterosexual, middle/upper-classed, Christian, able-bodied perspective'. Clearly clergy misconduct is precisely the subject area where such traditional forms of enquiry are not only inadequate but run the risk of reinscribing oppression, and where the so-called objectivity of academic enquiry must be problematised. Indeed, we may ask whether academic research is ever truly objective; without a keen investment in the subject who would engage in the work? Autoethnography allows writers to resist theoretical abstractions and to focus on the particulars of individual experience. It legitimises the specificity and uniqueness of individual emotional responses to, and cognitive interpretations of life events and socio-cultural contexts as valid data for research. In short, it values the way individuals find meaning (Benton 2013, 180; Fletcher 2018, 43). It locates the study of the self (often focussing on significant memorable events, existential crises, and life-changing occurrences) within an investigation of cultural relational practices, values, beliefs, and experiences (Ellis, Adams, and Bochner 2011, 2).

Autoethnography provides a helpful framework for processing trauma while simultaneously allowing the theologies and structures that perpetuate the trauma of individuals and groups to be exposed and critiqued. For many women, Shelly Rambo (2020, xvi) observes, 'the language and practices of Christian faith are *both* wounding and healing'. When we put real women into the frame and examine their experiences in the context of a theology and ecclesiology that continues to undermine them, and that makes women primarily responsible for sex, including sex that is coercive or non-consensual, we begin to gradually chip away at an edifice that has cloaked the liberating message of the gospel in a miserable shell of misogyny and dishonesty.

After nearly 30 years advocating for child victims of clergy abuse, David Clohessy (2018) comments that change only occurs when victims speak out. It can take decades for abuse victims to acknowledge and share or report their experiences. Sonja Grace's *Garlands from Ashes* (1996) told the stories of 15 women and three men who had been abused by church leaders in New Zealand as children, teenagers, or adults between 1940 and 1992. Remaining silent, Grace observes (p. 67), maintains the offender's power. More than this, it perpetuates the lie that clergy are beyond reproach and that churches are unequivocally safe environments. As with #MeToo, in finding the courage to tell their stories, the individuals in Grace's book not only found their own voices, they also empowered others to speak out and they exposed the truth about a human and flawed institution.

Mary Clark Moschella (2008, 9) makes a similar point regarding racism in an American Protestant church. An ethnographic study described by Moschella both exposed and neutralised the 'shameful secret' of racial prejudice in the congregation, thereby reducing its power. For Grace and those who shared their stories with her, speaking out was ultimately healing and empowering. For Moschella (pp. 5–7), ethnography – the study of human beings in their social and cultural contexts – becomes a form of pastoral practice in which narrative models of theology and pastoral care help others to find meaning, authority, and transformation in the telling and retelling of their personal stories. This is certainly true of my own experience and has practical consequences for the way my life is now unfolding. I say more about this in the concluding chapter.

As Kim Benton (2013, 171) notes, 'life-stories or narratives are by necessity retrospective in the shaping or ordering of past experience'. Reflecting on personal narratives helps us to make meaning, not only of our own lives but also of those of the people around us and our interactions with them. For Megan Fletcher (2018, 42–43), a retrospective autoethnographical analysis of her experience of intimate partner violence signified a return to feminist agency and empowerment. In contributing her personal story to the academic literature on intimate partner violence, which is largely theoretical due to the reluctance of survivors to publicly recount their experiences, she is grounding that body of knowledge in the reality of lived experience – helping others to understand why, for example, it is so hard to leave an abusive partner.

Autoethnography and narrative methodologies allow the researcher to engage interpersonally with the stories of active participants in their research and with stories related by fellow researchers. In hearing and reading the stories of others, I review, shape, and reshape my own experiences as my understanding increases and my frame of reference expands (Benton 2013, 170). In reading of the experience of five contemplative nuns who had been abused by priests, for instance (Durà-Vilà, Littlewood, and Leavey 2013), I am prompted to consider the more immediate effects that my own experiences of clergy misconduct had. The emotional content of these experiences has faded over time, and I realise that to an extent, I had either downplayed their consequences or failed to adequately identify them.

As I read of the shock, the tears, the anger, the fear, the spiritual turmoil of these nuns, I recall my much younger self walking out of a church during Communion in confusion and anger as the reality of my first experience of a priest violating a pastoral boundary hit me. As a young woman, I was shocked at the behaviour of a trusted authority figure, and it shook my faith in the church as the institution that had been most deeply formative of my worldview. Next, I am mindful of the irony of regaining consciousness on a hospital trolley vomiting gin and sleeping tablets into a bowl held by a priest whose coercive behaviour had profoundly undermined my ability to trust my own strength and resources or to prioritise my own well-being over his and had drawn me away from meaningful sources of support. Then, I contemplate the neck-pain and frequent migraines that remind me regularly of a violent physical assault by a well-connected, white, middle-class, Oxford-educated priest nearly 20 years ago. In refusing to keep the secret of this particular priest (a repeat abuser), mine, like Fletcher's (2018), becomes a resistant story in a discursive patriarchal, religious, and social context that typically prefers to assign gender violence to other classes and ethnicities – and certainly to other professions. Such was the confidence of this particular man in his white, middle-class, priestly respectability that he was able to deliver a radio broadcast on conflict resolution in Northern Ireland, whilst acting out his own capacity for violence in his personal life.

Through this engagement with the stories of other women and with my own, and through the considered telling and retelling of my story, autoethnography allows me to both reconstruct and transform (Fletcher 2018) my journey. There is now a purpose to what has hitherto felt like a pointless waste – of time, of vocation, of talents and competencies, of emotional resources, and precious moments I could have spent focussing on my children. As I reclaim my own agency in the way this story develops and resolves, I can see the value, not of the abuse itself – but of my experience and my understanding of it – as a resource for others. It was what it was, I am unable to change that. But I can now make the best of it. In describing her own rationale for telling her story of childhood sexual abuse in a theological college worship setting, Elizabeth Martin (2020, 11) comments:

> The key time Jesus told his own story, was his story of resurrection after a horrendous journey of abuse, torture and execution. Jesus tells his own story to the disciples as he appears to them, as he showed them his wounds, his scars (John 20:24–29). He

embodies his painful journey, but he shares his scars in the context of healing.

Martin chooses to reveal her scars to demonstrate that healing is possible and to assert that churches have a role in facilitating this. In sharing her story of abuse, she notes, those present who had also experienced abuse felt supported and less alone, while those who had not had their eyes opened to the lived experience of it. In sharing her story with trainee priests, she helped them prepare for ministry (p. 20).

This study tells my story and allows other women who have experienced clergy misconduct to tell theirs. As Grace (1996, 167–168) notes, telling these painful and often shaming stories can be cathartic provided they are heard empathically. Sadly, the lived experience of many women who have disclosed abuse, sought help from churches, and confronted or exposed their abusers is that the process at best does next to nothing and at worst compounds the abuse. The compassion, understanding, fair treatment, and justice they anticipate within an institution that claims to be Christ-centred and loving is suddenly and dramatically lacking when the person in the firing line is a member of the church hierarchy, and the complainant is the victim of a sexual offence. Some women have continued in ministry after experiencing clergy abuse. Some left the church because it was too painful and damaging a place to remain. Others were forced to abandon their long-held dreams of priesthood and watch while their abusers retained their dog collars, their stipends, and their privileged access to other trusting individuals at vulnerable times in their lives.

Much of the content of this volume will resonate with women in all denominations. New Zealand was one of the first countries to ordain women to the priesthood, and other provinces in the Anglican Communion have looked to it for insight and guidance in the area of gender and leadership. As the Anglican Church in Aotearoa, New Zealand, and Polynesia revises its misconduct policies, in part in response to the Royal Commission of Inquiry into Abuse in Care, the experience, mistakes, and attempts to do better in this microcosm of the church might serve to inform and enlighten the practice of other provinces and denominations. An explanatory note about the structure of the church in this province is necessary: In 1992, a constitutional change restructured the Anglican Church in the province of New Zealand into three separate, self-determining 'tikanga' or cultural streams: Tikanga Māori, Tikanga Pākehā, and Tikanga Pasifika. Each tikanga is headed by an archbishop. The province was designated the Anglican Church in Aotearoa, New Zealand, and Polynesia/Te Hāhi Mihinare ki Aotearoa, ki Niu Tīreni, ki Ngā Moutere o Te Moana Nui a Kiwa. The province's seminary, the College of St John the Evangelist/Hoani Tapu te Kaikauwhau i te Rongopai (St John's College), was restructured to reflect this. I confine my discussion in this volume to the church in the geographical area of Aotearoa New Zealand.[11]

Chapter outline

The rest of this volume unfolds as follows:

Using autoethnography as a springboard to a wider conversation in Chapter 2, I will draw on my own experiences of the Anglican Church in New Zealand and the UK, and those of other women, to illustrate theoretical perspectives on clergy sexual abuse: typical patterns followed by abusers, common responses from churches, and similarities in consequences for survivors. There is a consensus that institutional abuse only changes when survivors come forward. This chapter situates the authentic accounts of survivors of clergy misconduct in the broader context of vocation, leadership, and power in the church.

Chapter 3 begins with a description of the context in which I first experienced clergy misconduct: the Anglican Church in New Zealand in the 1980s. I explore the prevailing sexism that dominated the discourse on women's ministry and obstructed the call for inclusive language and a wider range of images for God. I argue that a broadly sexist and misogynist expression of gender and religion has contributed to rape culture in the church and enabled clergy abuse of women. I then explore whether this has changed. Given that women have been ordained in the Anglican Church in Aotearoa New Zealand for over 40 years, has the transformation that many hoped would accompany a more inclusive leadership actually happened? Extending the discussion beyond New Zealand Anglicanism, I consider the impact of clericalism and purity culture as maintaining discourses of rape culture in the church. These, I argue, perpetuate an environment where clergy abuse can thrive. While #ChurchToo has begun to challenge this culture with some success, there is much yet to do.

Chapter 4 explores the way forward, suggesting that alternative models for institutional Christianity are needed if the church is to address the problem of clergy sexual misconduct and give greater priority to the abused.

A number of people generously agreed to be interviewed for this project or were happy for me to share their stories, which are already in the public domain. Among them are clergy, church educators, survivors of misconduct or abuse by clergy, and those who have experienced other forms of abuse or prejudice in the church. In several cases, these categories overlap. Their stories, and/or their responses to the abuse crisis in the church contribute in significant ways to the following chapters. They speak more than adequately for themselves and their comments have therefore required little analysis from me. Where I use Christian names only, their names have been changed to protect their identities. I begin the next chapter by outlining the development of my vocation to ministry in the Anglican Church, before moving on to my experience of clergy misconduct.

Notes

1 See https://metoomvmt.org/.
2 See Clough (2017) for a discussion of Ireland's Magdalen laundries. In 2020, Margaret Wilkinson and Mrs D gave evidence to New Zealand's Royal Commission into Abuse in Care about abuse, including the forced adoption of their babies, they experienced in the 1960s at St Mary's Home for Unwed Mothers, run by the Anglican Trust for Women and Children.
3 Fiduciary duty is the legal or ethical obligation of a person with a duty of care or in a professional relationship of trust to act in the best interest of their client, congregant, or counselee.
4 See 'Common contributing factors across religious institutions' at https://www.childabuseroyalcommission.gov.au/religious-institutions [accessed 18.5.2021] re. clericalism, and IICSA 2018, 6–8.
5 The Māori name for New Zealand, which often precedes or replaces the English name.
6 Summarised at https://www.abuseincare.org.nz/reports/ [accessed 4.4.2021].
7 See law professor and survivor Julie Macfarlane's (2021) account of seeking restitution in the Church of England, for example.
8 See Zimbardo (2008) for a discussion of the systemic nature of abuse.
9 The Diocese of Nelson attempted to use this argument to assert that Michael van Wijk, who abused Thompson, was employed by God, not the church, and as such was not the church's responsibility (Johnston 2020). This claim has been used successfully by churches in employment disputes (for example, Mabon v. Methodist Church Conference, New Zealand, 1998).
10 The House of Bishops (2019, 5) asserts that marriage between a man and a woman 'remains the proper context for sexual activity'.
11 The Diocese of Polynesia (Tikanga Pasifika) comprises episcopal regions in Fiji, Tonga, and Samoa.

2 #MeToo

Beginning my story

Viewed with the hindsight of several decades and from a feminist perspective, my journey in the Anglican Church was not one that was likely to end happily. Indeed, for a girl child born in New Zealand in 1961, the idea of having a settled domestic life *and* a successful career in the church was perhaps a little ambitious. The former was certainly modelled to me, although I found the notion of it frustratingly restrictive. The latter was not. For a girl in the 60s with a vocation to priesthood, there were no models. So where had it come from?

My parents had met when my father was assigned to visit my mother during a stewardship campaign at their parish church in Stratford, a small farming town in Taranaki, New Zealand. They were married in 1960 and I was born 16 months later. When I was four years old, our family moved to Hamilton, a city at the heart of rural Waikato. Committed and active Anglicans, we joined our local parish church, moving to the Cathedral when my father joined the choir.

The story of my vocation began aged around seven or eight, with my conviction that when I grew up, I would be a priest. Not just a priest. A dean. I was very quickly told that role was not open to me because I was female. Undeterred, I announced to the Dean of St Peter's himself that I intended to be the first 'lady dean' at the Cathedral. I eventually succumbed to the notion that ordination was not an option for me but continued to be an enthusiastic churchgoer, even when my parents gave up the weekly battle to force my brother and sisters to go to church, and despite the fact that my school friends thought it was not cool. Inspired perhaps by Audrey Hepburn,[1] I was fascinated by nuns and by the Eucharist and badgered my parents and our parish clergy throughout my childhood to let me be confirmed, even asking to convert to Catholicism so that I could receive Communion.[2] I had a

DOI: 10.4324/9781003164937-2

strong pastoral streak as a child and regularly befriended and visited older people in our neighbourhood.

I continued attending church through my teens, singing in the Cathedral choir, serving, assisting with Sunday School, and attending the parish youth group. With a love of liturgy, I was drawn to the Prayer Book services and the ritual and incense that accompanied them, staunchly resisting the pull of the charismatic movement in the 1970s, although I secretly enjoyed the guitar-led praise songs. At my Anglican secondary school, we had daily chapel services and weekly Divinity classes, which I loved. In my final year or so, a visit from an English Anglican religious sister sparked the realisation that the Religious Life was an option for me, even though I was not Catholic.

The first women priests were ordained in New Zealand in 1977. I knew nothing of it. The following year I found myself in the chancel at the Cathedral in my role as a server, as two women were ordained deacon. The next morning, my vocation surfaced again as it dawned on me that ordination was now a possibility; I was no longer excluded from priesthood on gender grounds. I decided to study English literature at Otago University, with the intention of then doing a post-graduate Bachelor of Divinity, which appealed due to its heady combination of Greek, Hebrew, Biblical Studies, Church History, and Systematic Theology.

My initial attempts to explore this path again met with acute resistance to the ordination of women. While I did, of course, receive support from a number of Anglicans, including those who sent me to St John's College for ordination training, the people who responded enthusiastically to my calling were often either non-church-goers – people who had little time for the church but could clearly see me in that role – or members of denominations which already ordained women.

Jumping forward to recent years, two encounters led to my writing this volume. In the first, I connected on social media with a friend I had not been in touch with since the late 1980s. Living on opposite sides of the world, we arranged to skype. As I reflected on the conversation afterwards, it struck me that my friend spoke primarily about his life as a vocational journey. Family and relationships were present in his discourse, and indeed contained the story in a sense, but ministry provided the structure, the direction of movement. In contrast, despite not intending to, I spoke more of relationships and their effects on my life.

After our talk, I felt unsettled. I had wanted to give a positive account of my working life. Instead, I had related the story of a series of difficult relationships that had, at times, taken my energy and attention away from the things that really matter to me: my children, my creativity, and my work. I did not feel good about the story I told my friend. He and I met at theological college. We both set out with the same goal – a life in Christian ministry. He stayed on that path. I strayed. What went wrong?

The second encounter was with a chaplain from an Oxford college. I asked about her journey in the church. The story of her vocation could not have been more different from mine. Whereas I had first experienced my vocation to the priesthood as a child, the initial burst of enthusiasm and clarity quietening into a 'still small voice' that has persisted despite years of denial, frustration, and doubt, she had grown up never once thinking to be ordained. Her vocation was discerned not by her, but by others. The opposition that I had experienced had come, for her, not from outside, but from within; her response to the suggestion that she consider ordination was, 'you must be joking'. When she asked me, in turn, about my journey, I found myself unable to speak what I still experienced as a narrative of trauma, failure, and shame, and instead fobbed her off with a cliché: 'it's a long story'. Trauma, Lisa Spriggens observes (2018, 213) 'takes us beyond language', while gendered violence 'acts to silence victims/survivors and those who witness their stories through fear, shame, disbelief, blame, ridicule and exclusion'. To re-enter my own story in that moment was too risky.

What led to our paths being so different? I can easily believe this friendly, confident woman would have appeared to others to be eminently suitable for ministry. It is easy to look back and think, I just did not have what it takes. I was too secular in my expression, too reserved in articulating my faith, probably too flippant at times. I was certainly no evangelist. What is more, I was increasingly theologically and socially liberal, outspoken on issues that mattered to me, an anathema to those of a more evangelical or fundamentalist bent. Yet, underneath this was a serious faith, and from a young age, I was an active, committed Anglican.

On retrieving my student file from the archives of my theological college library, I am reminded that my referees commented on my 'compassion, real care and concern for people', my 'gifted ministry to the elderly', my 'low key but strong faith', and my 'uncompromising honesty in both a moral and intellectual sense'. My tutor at the college described me as 'an able and highly conscientious student', a 'sensitive leader of worship', and a 'young woman with many gifts'. The warden's annual reports express satisfaction with my academic results, and comment on my 'many qualities of character and spirituality', my 'depth of commitment to a caring ministry' and my 'passionate concern for inclusiveness ... in the life of the church, and of the language of worship and the communication of faith'.

These reports also note some of the factors that, in hindsight, would have made me vulnerable to clergy misconduct: a lack of confidence, undue anxiety over the quality of my work, sensitivity to sexist language and the androcentric nature of Anglican worship, theology, and life in the college and wider church. Significantly my tutor noted that as a young woman entering full-time ministry I would have 'few, if any, peers'.[3] She continued: 'She has much to offer the church, but I feel the effectiveness of her ministry will depend to a large extent on the support which she herself receives'.

On reading my file after an interval of over three decades, I am forced to re-evaluate the distorted negative self-perception I have developed in the intervening years and to more critically examine the broader context I had found myself in as a young ordinand in a church which had begun ordaining women only ten years earlier, and where an offer of 'counselling' from an older male priest had effectively stopped me accessing the support I needed.

I had been taught during confirmation preparation to approach theological matters critically and that there were multiple ways of reading scripture, a perspective I found liberating and which gave me tools to respond to the doubts that pervaded the era, and which I periodically personally experienced. For me, these episodes of uncertainty about my faith tended to coincide with the actions by the church or its members that I found hard to accept, especially if justice issues were at stake. Opposition to women's ordination across the Anglican Communion and to homosexuality are obvious examples. I held in tension a strong sense of vocation – that God was calling me to the priesthood – and a distrust of the church. Additionally, there were aspects of the church's teachings that I could not believe in any literal sense, even when I was younger. At times, I doubted the existence of God, but this perhaps had more to do with the limited language and imagery available at the time. Once this expanded and I allowed my own innate perception of the divine more space, God was more present than not. In 1990, after a particularly difficult and desolate time before I left the religious life, I had an unexpected and almost tangible experience of God that has never left me.

While it was not uncommon for more conservative or fundamentalist Christians to begin academic theological studies and experience shock and anger when some of their foundational beliefs were challenged, I found theological studies engaging, intellectually stimulating, and very liberating. I was fortunate to have some excellent lecturers both at Knox Theological Hall and at St John's College. Their teaching made Christianity available to me in a way that the church, on the whole, had not. However, there were gaps.

Reflecting on the requirements of clergy training in the mid-1990s, Brian Davis (1995, 77) states that the training of priests to be sacramental people must encompass spiritual development, skills to enable mission and to defend and promote Christian faith, and 'the development of relational skills'. However, he goes on to suggest that:

> [i]f a theological college is providing for the spiritual and social growth of future priests through regular worship and intimate community life, and is ensuring that its students are involved in serious theological exploration, it is my view that it need not be concerned if it is doing little more than this.

The 'practical skills in ministry' can, he says, 'be learned in the dioceses and parishes after ordination'. When I look back on my ordination training, what was lacking was precisely what Davis (who was then my diocesan bishop) suggested was not important for the college to provide: the practical skills needed for ministry. To my mind, these include training on professional standards and ethics. At the end of my training, I was theologically literate and could read the Bible in Greek and Hebrew, but I did not feel adequately prepared for parish ministry. Additionally, after two years in a Christian community that often felt like a battle ground, my confidence was low and my mental health was, at times, precarious.

I look back at the struggle of being young, female, single, and theologically liberal at St John's College in 1987, an environment that was much more suited to men and where, as women, our right to be there as ordinands was regularly challenged by some students. Unlike the stories I hear now, where support was offered and decisions about future ministry were taken with sage advice, I look at the constantly shifting goal posts and the inappropriate conversations about my future, by three male clergy over a game of tennis, for instance, and I cannot help but feel the church failed me.

I was nearing the end of my training with no clear idea of my future, strongly drawn to the religious life, terrified of not being a good enough priest, and endeavouring to take myself out of a situation with an older male priest that he should never have instigated. At the end of my two years at theological college, I left New Zealand with a scholarship to explore my vocation to the religious life and complete my studies abroad, with the aim of returning a year later with more clarity about my future path. I spent a month living in community with a contemplative religious order in Australia *en route* to the UK, where I received an enthusiastic welcome and was given a date for my ordination to the diaconate the following year, the bishop there having negotiated my transfer to that diocese. I was shocked, on my return, to find the community in conflict and fragmenting, to encounter hostility from the mother house in the UK, where women's ordination, even to the diaconate, was still controversial, and to discover that procedural goal posts within the diocese had shifted and my ordination was to be delayed. It was not a happy time, and I left the community nearly a year later feeling fragile and disillusioned.

Some years later, a priest colleague in the UK observed that what I had lacked in my journey towards ordination was any effective mentoring. He was correct. The few women clergy I knew were engaged in their own struggles in what was often a difficult and at times actively hostile environment. From my early twenties, until I left the church aged 41, I encountered several older male clergy who, while ostensibly supporting me in my vocation, had proved to be at worst predatory and at best lacking in professional boundaries. Those encounters were distracting and profoundly disorientating. Ironically, the priest who pointed out the lack of tangible clerical support proved to be similarly motivated.

In 2019, I returned to St John's College as a Visiting Scholar. At the end of that time, I wrote the following:

> Reconnecting with a friend who is an astute and experienced psychotherapist and spiritual director, I have the same problem discussing my experience of the church as I did when asked about it by the chaplain. Much of the story she knows already, but she patiently listens as I retell it, still struggling to make sense of it. It continues to feel messy, hesitant, and exposing.
>
> At our second meeting a few weeks later, we touch on the story again. In those few weeks, much feels resolved. My time at St John's has been healing. My research has fleshed out the context I found myself in. Other women had similar experiences. It was not just me. There is a shared history. A friend speaks of being 'crushed' by her early experience of ministry, and of that time setting the agenda for the next 25 years. Yes, I think, that is what happened for me too. At the time I trained there was only one ordained Anglican woman in New Zealand under 30 (Wood 1988, 2). I look back on my young self with more kindness and greater

understanding of dynamics that were too complex for me to grasp at the time. Despite this, I am still in a tangle as we discuss my vocation and what that means for my life now and in the future. Her take on it is that I was 'deeply traumatised' by my experience of the church. It is time, she thinks, for me to take my vocation out of the box in which I very consciously placed it some years ago and explore what it now means.

This volume is the product, and the process, of that exploration. In placing myself back in the location of a major experience of clergy misconduct at a formative time in my life and Christian ministry, I allowed my memories, spirituality, and vocation their freedom. With the maturity of age, 30 years of motherhood, and a career that has including teaching professional ethics to future health professionals, I reassessed my experiences of clergy misconduct with a new appreciation of their impact.

Sexual misconduct in the Anglican Church in New Zealand

In 1989, the first national conference of ordained Anglican women in New Zealand was held. A confidential workshop on sexual harassment offered at the conference was attended by nine women and subsequently attracted media attention. A journalist reporting on the conference was surprised to learn that such a workshop was considered necessary and decided to investigate further. According to Anglican priest Louise Deans (2001, 54), the workshop had been included in the programme to 'initiate a conversation about a problem [women] knew existed in the structures of the church, but which had not been talked about publicly'. Deans was not present at the conference but mentions that the nine women who attended the workshop 'were afraid of the consequences for their careers in the church' if the details of their discussion were disclosed, and for this reason it was agreed to keep the content of the workshop confidential.

The media attention that followed was the first time the problem of sexual harassment by clergy in New Zealand had been publicly disclosed (Deans 2001, 55). Deans, then newly priested, was among a number of women who alleged that they had been sexually abused by an Anglican clergyman, Canon Rob McCullough, in the years leading up to the conference.[4] Because she had not been present at the meeting and was not bound by confidentiality to that group, she agreed to speak anonymously to the press despite her concerns that her career in the church would be jeopardised. The immediate response from the church hierarchy was telling. Deans was contacted by her diocesan bishop who blamed her for the abuse, cast aspersions on her character, and asserted that McCullough was a victim in this situation (p. 56). Archbishop Brian Davis, interviewed in *The Press*, 7 September 1989, announced that priests were 'red-blooded males' like other men and asserted that 'it took two to tango' (p. 57). The struggle Deans and the other victims of McCullough's alleged persistent and serial abuse had to be heard by members of the church hierarchy, who appear to have sided with McCullough, is detailed in her book *Whistle Blower* (2001) and was outlined by her for the Royal Commission of Inquiry into Abuse in Care in 2020. Bishop of Christchurch, Peter Carrell, stated in his evidence to the Royal Commission that McCullough had abused 'his power and influence over several women ... engaging in behaviour with them which was sexual harassment and/or sexual abuse' (Abuse in Care 2021a, 17:95).

I was not aware of these revelations, having left New Zealand a year earlier, and wonder whether I would have made the connection with my own experience of clergy misconduct had I been. Despite the protestations the previous year of a friend who was aware of the way a certain priest was 'winding himself around me' as she recently put it, I was still of the belief that the situation I found myself in was my responsibility. With the hindsight of 34 years, a career in a 'helping' profession with clear ethical standards outside the church and significantly more awareness of the dynamics of sexual harassment and abuse than I had back then when it was seldom talked about, I can now look back on the way I was drawn into an emotional dependency with a priest who was older than my father and see it for what it was.

Grooming strategies

As a 25-year-old candidate for ordination, I had been subjected to a protracted period of grooming. This common characteristic of clergy abuse is a process –

> whereby the religious leader breaks down a woman's defenses, making her feel special – perhaps by pointing out her spiritual gifts – or in other ways using his position as a religious leader to develop a close relationship with her and isolate her from others.
>
> (Garland 2013, 123)

Marie Fortune (1999) summarises the similarities in the grooming strategies used by the clergy abusers of the six women who tell their stories in Nancy Werking Poling's book *Victim to Survivor* – stories that Fortune notes 'can be multiplied by the thousands in North America and around the world' as follows: 'He made her feel special; he took her seriously, she thought; he mentored her in her vocation for ministry; he isolated her from other people' (pp. ix, xi). In my experience, all this was true.

I can see now that this priest reeled me in to meet his own needs, on the pretext of offering me counselling when I was going through a difficult time. When I felt the counselling was no longer necessary, he persuaded me to keep seeing him. At this point I had expressed my concern about becoming dependent on his support. I trusted his experience and professionalism when he batted my concern away. Some months later, during a period of acute stress before my end of year exams, he announced that he had been in love with me since he first saw me. In the sessions that followed, he began speaking about his depression and issues in his marriage.

From her account, it appears McCullough had taken a similar approach with Deans (2001, 32–33, 35) who also found herself isolated by his actions. Deans comments that when he began talking to her about his marital problems, their roles reversed, and she became the 'carer' of his welfare. This kind of role reversal is a common element in the grooming process (Stephenson 2016, 39). Like Deans, I was a natural carer. My vocation always had a strongly pastoral impulse, and this aspect was easily appealed to. Describing the process of grooming, Anne Stephenson (2016, 19) states that there is 'inappropriate personal sharing by the sexual predator so that the victim feels like the counsellor and is consequently the protector of his vulnerability'.

With this now mutual sharing, our relationship moved into one of friendship (at least, that was how I interpreted it), and in an environment where I frequently felt stressed and, at times, under attack, such friendship was welcomed. Having grown up in a household where clergy became family friends who we socialised with regularly, this progression in our relationship seemed a natural one. When he took me out for lunch to celebrate the end of my exams, I felt cared for. He was not the first older clergyman to treat me to lunch, so I did not query the rightness of it. However, when social invitations escalated, I followed the advice of a friend to put boundaries in place and asked him not to contact me. Shortly afterwards, he made a serious suicide attempt. I shifted into looking-after mode. I cared about what happened to him. Having tried, and failed, to reset the boundaries with someone who was clearly vulnerable, I took responsibility for what ensued.

Some months later, his bishop was made aware of our friendship. There was a facilitated attempt at resolving things, but it was poorly handled. We reached an agreement to stop meeting. It was unrealistic and the contact simply became clandestine. The facilitating priest offered to support me to manage the situation. At our first and only meeting he announced that he hoped he 'didn't fall in love too, as he tended to do so'. Deans (2001, 45) describes her attempt to seek professional help in the Christchurch diocese. The priest she confided in informed her that 'the type of behaviour I had described to him was commonplace for men in the church and that he himself had engaged in similar relationships. He said that there was nothing wrong with it, in fact it was rather fun'. The Sunday after these ostensibly confidential meetings, a member of the church pastoral team rushed up to me after the morning service to tell me how well I had managed the situation. The facilitator had revealed the details of the meetings, and our identities, to her.

Sexual contact, when it eventually happened, was thankfully short-lived. I was not remotely attracted to him, but it was sought by him in such a way that eventually I caved in. Then, with the stress I was under as an academic deadline approached and with a lack of support from other quarters due to my increasing isolation, the dependency he was encouraging took shape.

This relationship occupied most of my two years at theological college. I remember the realisation, one spring afternoon, that the only way to extract myself from this man, who was clearly infatuated with me, was to leave the country. While that was not my only reason for going, it certainly played its part. And with some distance, my perspective got sharper and I made the break – forbidding any further correspondence and refusing to respond when it came anyway. Sporadically over the years attempts to communicate were renewed and at one point, out of compassion to a man who was by then elderly, I replied.

Characteristics of clergy abuse

I am still reluctant to describe what this kind, gentle man did as abuse, yet the more I research this area, the more I understand that indeed it was. Whether he had intended it or not, it was a profound and protracted violation of professional boundaries. As much as I would like to believe otherwise, his extensive, international professional training and experience in ministry is evidence that he, more than many other locally trained clergy at the time, must have known this.

All the typical elements of professional misconduct were there. The sustained period of grooming, disclosure of his marital problems and personal unhappiness, the need for secrecy, through which I was increasingly isolated, the coercion to have sex which was clearly premeditated; he had bought contraception. His several professional roles in relation to me placed him in a position of power and trust. Where I finally gave in to his repeated requests for intimacy thinking it was so little to ask, I now have a clear view of the cost – to my psychological well-being, my sense of self and not least, to my vocation to ministry. Looking back now from the perspective of a mother of daughters the age I was then, I feel both anger and grief at the unboundaried, unprofessional, and entirely self-interested way that priest behaved.

Why do women fall for it?

Such scenarios, I now understand, set the agenda for the events that followed. Older male clergy were modelling relationships that breached professional boundaries and duty of care – and no one was stopping them. Even comments and interactions that may have seemed trivial at the time were paving the way for more egregious boundary violations. These unprofessional practices were being normalised by mature, experienced, and respected church leaders, and further legitimised by those of their colleagues and bishops who knew something of their behaviour but were not offering a critique, let alone acting to prevent it happening again.[5] I do not recall any input on professional ethical standards during my ordination training that would have prompted me to make the connections with this behaviour. This priest had both encouraged dependency and created an unhealthy precedent, leaving me vulnerable to exploitation by other clergy.

I am certain that I would never have entered that relationship had it not unfolded in the way it did, had my vulnerability not been taken advantage of by a man with power and responsibility some 30 years my senior whom I regarded as almost a father figure. It simply would not have occurred to me. Commenting on the way women take responsibility for clergy abuse and accept the abuser's narrative that the relationship is consensual, Garland (2013, 126) notes that when confronted with the question would she have become involved if he were her neighbour, not her pastor – women almost invariably say no. A priest's power and authority make meaningful consent with a congregant impossible. This question has been most helpful for me in deciphering where I did and did not have full agency with male clergy. I now believe that if I had received appropriate support from a skilled mentor or supervisor, and some authentic counselling or psychotherapy during my training, the outcome would have been different, and I may well have made a useful contribution to ordained ministry in the Anglican Church in New Zealand.

It is easy now, to look back on that episode in my life and ask myself why I fell for it. Peter Rutter (1989, 91) explains that when a woman puts her trust in a male therapist who later attempts to sexualise the relationship, she 'by deep inner training, is preadapted to numbly turn over her body and sexuality to his needs'. This certainly resonates. I clearly remember thinking at the time, 'it's so little to ask'. Equally, it was an act that gave me no pleasure and I soon realised it had been a mistake.

A survivor of clergy misconduct writes of her experience:

> You think it's not a big deal and somehow their need outweighs anything else. And then the intimacy takes hold and you're stuck in it. You're in a dichotomy or a double bind. On the one hand knowing you shouldn't be there for all sorts of ethical and practical reasons: the potential and actual effects on others (your family, his family, the wider church family) and being out of step with the church's teaching. It conflicts with your principles as a Christian and a feminist and you even recognise some of his behaviour as abusive. On the other hand, you get hooked into what the relationship gives you: intimacy, a quality of attention that is lacking elsewhere, affirmation of your vocation, practical and emotional support ... you live in the polarity. It's a hugely uncomfortable and confusing place to be and it takes a lot of energy.

Another feature of clergy abuse is that women are usually drawn into such relationships during vulnerable times in their lives. We succumb when there is a chink in our armour, when we have been destabilised by stress or trauma, by conflict, bereavement, rejection, or exhaustion.

My susceptibility to getting hooked the first time a priest, an excellent mentor until that point, crossed the professional boundary was minimal. I was flattered that this charismatic man more than twice my age, in the role I had aspired to since childhood, felt able to confide in me about his marriage breakdown (ironically, enough to tell me he had hit his wife – 'she just wouldn't shut up'). I was probably flattered when he embraced me on the vicarage steps, even though I was not physically attracted to him. I was certainly caught up in the heady excitement of the vicar, who was popular with my housemates, singling me out. But when my next contact with him was an effusive letter claiming that he would kill himself if I did not run off with him, I was horrified. I gave the letter to my father, who assured me the threat was not serious and advised me to ignore it, which I did. My father was right.

I had promptly put a stop to this situation. The consequence for me, however, was huge. I was so disturbed by the letter that I left the congregation in which I had been actively involved and struggled to find my way to another. In a short space of time and out of the blue, I had lost my worshipping community, a valued mentor, and valuable experience for ministry. The congregation had lost a young person who had filled several roles in the church and who regularly visited older parishioners. I struggled to find another church to belong to in the diocese, although I was still actively involved in my family's congregation during holidays. Despite my telling the diocesan bishop the reason I had left, he would not engage in a conversation about my vocation while I was not settled in a parish and he made no effort to support me to safely find another spiritual home in the diocese.

Psychologically, I believed I had escaped from that situation relatively unscathed, thanks, in part, to my father assuring me that I was not responsible for the suicide threat. Beyond my age (about 21) and naivety, I was not particularly vulnerable at that point and was able to re-establish the boundaries of that relationship very quickly, albeit by walking away from it, and the congregation altogether. Subsequent events were different in that respect.

I did not receive any pastoral support regarding this incident, and it surprised me that, to my knowledge, neither of the clergy I have mentioned so much as had their 'knuckles rapped', let alone were any questions asked about their fitness to continue in their respective roles. And here it becomes complicated. The priest I have just mentioned was a good mentor until that boundary slipped. My journey may have been altogether different had it not. He was an enthusiastic and charismatic leader and went on to have a long and, what appears to have been, fruitful ministry. None of us are one-dimensional and we all make mistakes. Whether these were one-off incidents for these men, I do not know. I hope they were, although many abusers are repeat offenders (Rutter 1989, 41). Should they have been allowed to continue in ministry? If so, what support and supervision should they have been given? That they continued in their respective roles unchecked, despite their bishops having some knowledge of what had occurred was clearly negligent. An effective intervention in both cases could have prevented a great deal of harm.

Priests fall in love too

In a church that cannot cope with sex and hides from scandal, the complexities of human relationships and emotional pain are often overlooked. Furthermore, a church which is fighting to retain its patriarchal hierarchy is blind to abuses of power. If we generously assume that both these priests were good men who floundered once at difficult times in their own lives, but had otherwise valuable ministries, we must ask whether appropriate and timely interventions by the church leaders *who knew* could have led to a healthy outcome for all concerned. These situations could have been the basis for growth. But that would have required pastoral insight, a willingness to acknowledge institutional failings, and a commitment to the wellbeing of *all* parties. The boys' club that was the Anglican Church hierarchy in New Zealand in the 1980s was just not up to this, as Jane's story of her experience as an ordinand will demonstrate[6]:

> When I met Richard and we started to get to know each other I sensed there was something between us, but I wasn't going to acknowledge it or initiate a conversation – and he certainly didn't. There was a sort of dance really, where we both pretended that nothing was happening, but we'd find ourselves sitting next to each other at lunch or whatever, in a way that I thought could be coincidental.
>
> Neither of us knew what to do with those feelings. I was thinking, 'this is impossible. Nothing can happen.' He was married. He was faculty, I was a student. There was just nowhere, nowhere to go with the feelings.
>
> Much later when he reflected back on that period he'd say, 'look, I was completely in denial'. He was so stuck emotionally. He believed he'd tried everything he could to address the issues in his marriage. He was mindful that his 25th wedding anniversary was coming up. For him, that ought to be not just a celebration of the previous 25 years, but also a looking forward to the next 25 years. The idea of moving forward in that relationship was the equivalent of a death. He saw things starkly in terms of life and death, and it was crippling him.
>
> At the time, I was really confused, he was in denial, and yet we felt drawn to each other. So, we did what people do, we started to see each other in secret.
>
> Towards the middle of my second year when Richard had been separated for about six months, rumours were circulating, and I was summoned to the principal's office.
>
> He made some kind of accusation that I was seeing Richard, which, naturally, I denied. He then went into a big, long story about how getting romantically involved with Richard would be detrimental to my vocation because it would show a severe lack of judgment on my part, as he was so recently out of a marriage and

it would be a rebound relationship. He explained that such lack of judgment on my part would make me 'totally and permanently' unsuitable for ministry. I remembered the phrase because I was familiar with it from having worked in insurance.

He seemed to be pleading with me; he choked up as he told me a story about a couple whom he'd wholeheartedly supported to get married. The husband was, he later realised, on the rebound, and not too long afterwards the marriage broke down. I could only surmise that the break-up had caused him huge embarrassment for having endorsed the marriage, and that he'd been humiliated by its hasty demise.

I just sat there thinking, 'this is your problem', and as I recall, I left the meeting with no next steps, having experienced some mystifying behaviour for which there were no other witnesses. There was another meeting, where he advised me that he was going to write to my bishop recommending that they pull me from the programme on account of my 'total and permanent' unsuitability for ordained ministry and spelling out the terms on which I was to exit the college.

The letter that he sent me was quite draconian. I had about a month to clear out of my cloister flat, and there was a list of prohibitions: I wasn't allowed to go to the library, I wasn't to go to chapel, I wasn't to go to college lunches – or that communal space – and I wasn't allowed to go to classes. As it was the beginning of the semester the classes I was enrolled in were being cancelled, along with my allowance.

It was a friend who read the letter and said, 'he can't tell you that you're forbidden to go to chapel! The eucharist is open to all!' She made representation to him on my behalf, and he rescinded that bit. It became obvious to Richard and me that many of his actions had nothing to do with me, some of which came to light subsequently.

Meanwhile, Richard was summoned to a meeting with bishops and various people and was able to bring a colleague as a support person, and he was accused of having an inappropriate relationship with a student. The evidence they had for this was that when the two of us were in the same room, there were sparks between us.

So, they didn't actually know for a fact?

No. And the choice he was given was, 'you can resign, or we'll fire you'. They had this pretence of a meeting and made these accusations, but nothing was going to happen differently as a result of it, it was just going through the motions.

The principal used to tell us in Anglicanism classes, that in his day it was common to do what he did, which was to get into your first parish and to marry one of the young ladies of the parish. That was the mindset he came out of. In hindsight, I have no idea how Richard and I could have moved our relationship forward and still stayed within the framework of the church, whereby he could continue with his vocation and I could continue with my vocation. There was just no way.

It seemed that there was a no man's land between being single and being married. When you're getting into a relationship with somebody, you can't declare it. You don't know how it will develop. It's only really when you get engaged that you're making a public statement that the church can work with. You're making a public statement that this is a relationship with a future that we aspire to be within marriage. I wasn't prepared to sacrifice pursuing my sense of vocation for something that was still evolving.

It seemed to Richard that the principal had professional jealousies of him too. So once there was a whiff of something happening between Richard and me it seemed to incense him, and he wasn't able to think rationally or reasonably. I think he was humiliated that there was something happening on his watch that he'd been oblivious to.

I was really conscientious because at heart I'm a girly swot, and I was so aware that I'd only come into the Anglican Church in my late teens and had so much to learn. I was so naive when I think about it. The women in Christchurch, I had no idea about that. No idea about anything about sexual abuse.

That's really interesting. Given that had happened already and it was reported in the media, why wasn't that being dealt with at the college?

I don't recall anything about it at college. I presume it would have happened, if it was going to happen, in those Anglican formation classes that were outside the formal academic curriculum. That was when we had the principal just talking about meeting your wife when you do your curacy. All I remember from those classes was just him pontificating about things from a very 1950's world view.

So, no boundaries training?

No. No, not that I recall.

What was the impact on Richard's vocation?

Richard had sabbatical leave owing, but he was being hurried off the campus, so he found a place to move to. I left before him because it took a whole lot longer for him to find a place. I moved in with him two or three months later and we got married two years after that. Richard applied for other academic leadership roles offshore, but wasn't successful, and then he decided to go back to university and do more study. So, he did that and picked up some other work on the side.

We went to church regularly, and he preached and presided occasionally. Richard's license was never revoked. He always had a license to officiate in the diocese. His faith and his sense of vocation were never shaken, and he had more to offer. A role came up in another diocese after we'd been married over ten years, and the bishop supported Richard applying. One time when I was at the diocesan office, the bishop called me into his office and said that if I ever wanted to pursue a sense of priestly vocation, then 'his door was open'.

How did you feel about that?

I thought, 'you should be so lucky!' By that time, I had moved on so far it was not of interest. My girlfriend was reminding me the other day that Richard had said to her, 'Jane saved my life. I was in two unhealthy marriages, one with the mother of my children, and one with the church, and she rescued me'. It was from death to life, from darkness to light. His faith, his belief in the church, that was fine. He was able to separate out certain individuals with their human frailties and still believe in God and church.

How did he feel about what happened to you?

He was enormously empathetic towards me and he had huge confidence in my capabilities and thought that it was very much their loss. We both had a conviction that in our respective capacities we were doing the Lord's work. The vicar at our church, the church we were married at, asked me to be his warden and I was his warden for three years or so. I felt like he was saying, 'it stinks how you were treated, and this is a way I can acknowledge your competence.' I was also on the roster for leading worship. He gave me opportunities to feel validated in my vocation in that capacity.

What about your vocation – what happened to that?

It just ebbed away. My confidence took a hit. I'd really put myself out there, way out of my comfort zone, to pursue that sense of vocation. Had I not met Richard, I would have continued on in that vocation. Richard and I used to joke about what would have happened if I'd never have met him, and our answer – we were alluding to Somerset Maugham's short story, *The Verger* – was that I'd have been vicar of Fielding.[7] It was a machine, and it didn't have the robustness or whatever to accommodate our situation.

It being the church or it being the college?

I think the college, under that particular leadership.

Looking back at that situation now, how would you have handled it? How might it have been managed differently?

In retrospect, if there had been somebody safe who was independent, maybe within the diocese, maybe the ministry education person or someone like that, somebody safe that I could have gone to and said, 'hey there's a situation here but it's very sensitive and delicate', you can imagine. The same way that if in the middle of my training I'd decided I was transgender, but I didn't want to jeopardise my vocation. Someone safe, outside the college, that I thought would have had my back and I thought would have a pastoral concern for me.

The context was a relationship that was leading towards marriage. So, it's the real deal, it's long term, we've got the whole of our life's work and ministry on the canvas here. I would have taken a year or two years or whatever it was off, done something different and then re-engaged with the process. But that was never going to be an option for us. I mean I could have even carried on with my studies and taken time out of the ordination track or something.

So, there was no external process or person or supervision? Did you have a supervisor or a spiritual director?

I had a spiritual director. A Catholic nun. She was a nice, sweet lady but I really didn't understand what a spiritual director could or should be doing for me.

But not the sort of person you could have dealt with this issue with?

No. There was nobody safe.

And you didn't have anyone external who would have been safe you could have taken this to and worked through it? There was no one dealing with this in an adult fashion. That kind of professional supervision was not on offer?

You just don't know who to trust in that situation. You become paranoid.

I didn't get closure. That's what I realised. I never got closure. Richard did. He got a sense of closure about his time at the college. In divorcing his wife, he felt like it was a double divorce from the college. And his priestly vocation continued to be validated. He always was able to officiate and celebrate and preach, and he had another stint in parish ministry. And that validation for me? I just got kicked out. Yes, our vicar was kind to me and gave me that leadership opportunity within the congregation, but I've got half a degree in theology which is now out of limits so I can't finish that. I thought about it but actually I'd moved on. I didn't have the academic interest. I feel that my sense of vocation lies in a different area now. And my priestly vocation ebbed.

What would give you that sense of closure?

When I was with Richard, I felt like I didn't need it so much because our marriage and our shared sense of doing the Lord's work validated that. But now without him, there's nothing. There's no marriage, there's no vocation. I still feel like I'm drifting. I have nothing. I don't even have the degree. And it's a long time ago now.

The other thing I'd say is, this has more to do with Richard having passed away, I still feel strange going to Communion. When I go to church, I don't have a sense of place. With him, being married to him, that made sense of the church for me. But now when I go to church, I don't feel like I belong. I see the hope for my spirituality could well be through the Pihopatanga.[8] Because Tikanga Māori at college always stood outside of the politics and all that went down about us. They were always very non-judgmental and hospitable and quite appalled at what had happened.

I came out of a place where you just accepted things and you didn't think you had a voice. Louise Deans didn't feel she could speak up. That's absolutely the place that I came out of. You show your elders respect, and you don't answer back. My personality is to say nothing and retreat and try to work out what to do. But the point is the conditioning. You don't speak out, you don't embarrass someone in authority. I certainly had that level of deference to the principal and the bishop. I was really learning the ropes. There's no way I'd have felt confident to say to the principal when he was getting emotional and talking about this rebound relationship, there's no way I'd have said it's not appropriate for us to carry on talking. Because of that deference, I had been molested when I was younger and had experience of being violated, because I didn't realise that I could stand up for myself. I thought, what have I done to bring this on for myself. That's the go-to: I brought this on myself.

I identify with much in Jane's story, not least her sense of being adrift since Richard's death left her without an anchor or context for her own ministry. I worked hard over the years that I attempted to stay away from the church for my own well-being, to convince myself that my vocation lay elsewhere. Throughout that time, I held my antipathy for the church in tension with a strong sense of bereavement and loss.[9] Equally, I identify with Jane's closing comments. Like many other women of my generation, I grew up with a strong social conditioning around putting others before self, not challenging those in authority, not speaking up for oneself. I was conditioned to defer to those in authority, notably clergy, teachers, and medics, and had not been allowed, as a child, to set my own boundaries. There is a vulnerability that results from this.

The reaction to Jane and Richard's developing relationship was heavy-handed and ill-considered. There was no real process to manage this situation. There was no attempt to ascertain the nature of their relationship and to navigate an appropriate path, not even a meeting with both of them together, and certainly no pastoral process. Importantly, there was evidently no acknowledgement of the fact that, as a student and ordinand, Jane was in the care of the college and both the college and her diocese had a responsibility for her welfare.

Despite the fact that the Ordained Women's Conference had made a number of recommendations concerning sexual harassment and the need for training, and despite the McCullough case, there was no boundaries training at the college during Jane's time there, as far as she can recall – or certainly none that she associated with her own situation. This ongoing lack of education and training creates exactly the conditions where professional boundaries are overstepped, as there are few checks and balances. The rules are not clear.

Who pays?

Undisputedly, Richard had breached professional boundaries by becoming involved with a student. While intervention was necessary, this situation arguably warranted a more nuanced approach and with more thoughtful leadership it might have been handled compassionately and judiciously. Instead, Jane was expelled from the college and prevented from completing her training. In taking this path, neither the college nor the diocese exercised their duty of care.

In a context where the ethics of relationships, sex, and power are not robustly and wisely discussed, it is difficult to navigate these issues and to address such situations fairly and prudently when they do arise. This shortfall in education and training for both students and staff/ clergy creates extraordinary vulnerability.

As Jane observed, theirs was a context that was leading towards marriage. A more constructive way of managing their situation would, she suggests, have been for her to have taken time out, or perhaps finished her studies elsewhere. Equally, Richard was owed a sabbatical and in fact took this before his resignation took effect. This could have been an ideal opportunity for Jane to continue her training, allowing them both time to reflect, with appropriate supervision, on their circumstances and priorities, and for a more balanced course of action to be determined.

Archbishop Philip Richardson outlines a situation that had a more equitable outcome:

> *I'm wondering about situations where a priest and parishioner, for example, fall in love. Have you had to deal with situations like that?*
> Yes, absolutely. I can think of one particular example. It was a priest, who was the vicar of a parish and fell in love with a not long separated parishioner. I made it clear that that was clearly pastorally inappropriate. That, in effect, the pastoral relationship could not continue. So, the parishioner agreed to worship in a neighbouring parish. And not long after that, the priest moved to another position in another diocese. Not long afterwards the former parishioner followed the priest and they married, and they are still married. The discipline, I think, was clear. That in terms of disciplining ourselves [as clergy], in terms of our behaviour, you cannot offer ministry, particularly pastoral ministry to someone that you're in a relationship with.

Affair or abuse?

By his own admission in conversations during our protracted relationship, the priest I later became involved with in the UK targeted women at vulnerable times in their lives. He told me that work provided a good cover for his behaviour, and that he had previously engaged in similar relationships with an ordinand and with a parishioner who was going through a difficult divorce. He fitted the stereotype of a narcissistic personality described in the literature on clergy misconduct. Most such clergy, according to Fortune (2013, 16) 'are sociopathic and thus accomplished at manipulating the system in which they operate'. Citing a 1998 study by Friberg and Laaser, Diana Garland (2013, 122) suggests that 'the most common offender is a man who is reasonably successful and has a combination of narcissism, sexual compulsion, and need for affirmation'. This describes him well. This man did some creative work in the church. He also did profound harm. He was bright, talented, and energetic. He was also verbally and emotionally abusive and physically violent. When he moved to a new diocese, the onus to report his behaviour was left, by the bishop in the diocese he had moved from, up to me. I was recovering from a physical assault by this man who, more than once, had threatened to kill me and to kill my children if our relationship became public. Such disclosure on my part was not really on the cards.

Watching the BBC2 documentary on Church of England Bishop, Peter Ball, a prolific abuser of teenage boys and young men, I am struck by the culture of secrecy and obfuscation in the hierarchy of both church and the Establishment.[10] According to the investigating police officer Wayne Murdock, in 1992 when the first allegations were made against Ball, such a complaint against a bishop was unheard of. It was 2015 before Ball was finally charged for sexual offences against 18 teenage boys and young men. Watching senior church leaders, including former Archbishop of Canterbury, George Carey, ignore the allegations, actively withhold information from the police and excuse Ball's behaviour on the grounds that he had done a good job in the church and was repentant (so repentant that he continued to abuse) put my own experience in context. If the hierarchy were prepared to doggedly shield a serial abuser at the expense of his young victims, they were certainly not going to intervene in any meaningful way where the victim of abuse was an adult woman.[11]

I was a similar age to Louise Deans, and at a similar stage in family life with two young children, when I walked blindly into that situation. Feeling frustrated and isolated at home, I was in the middle of a messy divorce and a protracted period of stress. I had moved to a new city, where I knew almost no one, leaving good friends behind. We moved twice in four months, and I single-handedly nursed the children for weeks through whooping cough, measles, and chicken pox, leaving me sleep-deprived and exhausted. After five years at home parenting small children, my confidence was low and the last thing I wanted at that point was a job in the church, an institution I was by then strongly disaffected by. However, a job was advertised in a nearby parish, and we needed the extra income. Reluctantly, I went for an interview.

Ironically, when he opened the vicarage door, my first thought was 'I'm safe from this one'.

So it was that I found myself working with a priest who on the one hand insisted I should apply for ordination in the Church of England and on the other, it transpired, wanted a sexual relationship with me. As Deans (2001, 31) outlines her early meetings with McCullough, I am reminded of the early stages of that relationship, and the appeal of a man who, while not remotely physically attractive, was intelligent and charismatic. I admired his use of language, his theological perspective, and his enthusiasm. When he turned his mind to a pastoral situation, he could be skilfully present in a way that left one feeling astutely heard, and he injected intellectual clarity into complex situations. In a church that was often hostile to women's ordination, he was publicly committed to it, as he was to other justice issues.

As an experienced priest, he discerned my vocation and was affirming of my skills and experience in the parish and as a colleague. As a sexual predator, he was ultimately disrespectful of both my personhood and my vocation. It is not uncommon for victims of clergy sexual exploitation to interpret what is developing as an 'intimate bond or 'special' relationship' (Durà-Vilà, Littlewood, and Leavey 2013). What I failed to realise then was that our relationship was not 'an affair' – such was the discourse that accompanied it, but a profound breach of trust – and of the fiduciary duty attendant upon his roles as both my pastor and my employer. Certainly, neither the bishop nor the clergy who eventually came to know about the situation disabused me of that. Garland (2013, 123) observes that such mislabelling is common among professionals advising or supporting women victims of clergy sexual misconduct. Clearly it was convenient for the bishop to maintain the language of adultery rather than acknowledge that a priest he had been responsible for was guilty of serious professional misconduct.

Framing sexual misconduct as a sexual issue presupposes it is reciprocal and mutual. This positioning of clergy abuse serves both the abuser and the church leadership. When we reframe clergy misconduct as an abuse of power rather than of sexuality it allows the person who has been wronged to define the abuse, rather than giving that additional power to the abuser (Kleiven 2018, 277). While sex was obviously a factor in this relationship, what was problematic was the abuse of power by a priest in positions of responsibility relative to me. Added to that, he was coercive, controlling, and physically violent. His behaviour on a number of occasions was criminal.

Because I interpreted this unfolding situation as an affair, which implies a degree of mutuality and agency, I failed to fully recognise the abuse inherent in the game of cat and mouse that was being played with my emotions, and which quickly began to adversely affect my psychological wellbeing.[12] Garland (2013, 124) describes grooming as 'seduction' in a relationship in which the pastor holds spiritual power over his victim. Notably, the majority of respondents in a cross-denominational study of clergy abuse termed their experiences as 'romantic affairs' – even those involving physical violence or threats (Garland and Argueta 2010, 10). For Rocío Figueroa, sexual abuse by clergy is always preceded by spiritual abuse; by the manipulation of a person's faith and trust, achieved through the abuse of clerical power (Cathnews New Zealand 2020).

Prevalence of clergy abuse of women

It strikes me now that while I had attended church regularly for much of my life until 2003, the number of church communities I had been involved in was relatively small. Yet I had either experienced or witnessed some form of clergy misconduct in several of them. In one church, a priest had been intimate with several women in the congregation, all of whom were at vulnerable points in their lives. In another, two stipendiary clergy were sexually involved with congregants. And there were other church leaders I knew of who had so-called 'affairs' with individuals in their care. While it is hugely discomforting to feel like the common denominator in more than one episode of clergy misconduct, the snapshot of my life in the church alone suggests that such behaviour by clergy is by no means unusual.

Many cases of clergy misconduct are never reported, and the scale of abuse is hard to calculate. In 1984, doctoral researcher Richard Blackmon at Fuller Theological Seminary in California found that 39% of clergy across the four protestant denominations surveyed acknowledged having sexual contact with a congregant, while 76% knew of a pastor who had sex with a congregant (Schoener 2013, 9). The 2008 United States General Social Survey found that 'one in 33 women in congregations has been the object of a sexual advance by her religious leader' (Garland 2010, 3). Fortune (2013, 15) notes that research and media reports suggest that between 10% and 20% of clergy are guilty of sexual misconduct.

Prior to New Zealand's Royal Commission into Abuse in Care, there were no central records of clergy abuse in the Anglican Church in New Zealand. While some diocesan records were searched as the church prepared to give evidence at the Commission, it is my understanding that searches were restricted to records of the abuse of children or of vulnerable adults in the sense of adults who needed long-term health or social care.[13] Additionally, records were often scant and well hidden. In some cases, they were destroyed. In the course of giving evidence to the Commission, Bishop of Christchurch Peter Carrell (Abuse in Care 2021a(ii), 330–332) stated that individual bishops determined record-keeping policy and that primary documents pertaining to abuse cases in his diocese in recent years were shredded, with only final reports retained. Carrell was questioned about reports that Allan Pyatt, Bishop of Christchurch from 1966–1983, is thought to have had a bonfire before he retired, potentially destroying evidence for that period of time (ibid. 332).

The 1989 Ordained Women's Conference had requested national guidelines addressing sexual harassment in the church. Such was the secrecy surrounding abuse disclosures at this point in time, that the women involved in the McCullough case believed their situation to be unique (Allan 1996, 66). My story is evidence that it was not. Furthermore, 35 women, apart from Deans, were eventually to allege abuse by McCullough (Abuse in Care 2020a, 4). Also at that time, Catholic laywoman, Trish McBride alleged that she had been abused by 'Jim', a Methodist minister, and her boss at an interdenominational chaplaincy organisation. McBride's story began, like mine, in 1987 with an offer of support. Recently widowed and newly employed as a chaplain in the organisation Jim headed, McBride had just re-entered the workforce after a long break raising her six children. She was quickly lured by Jim into an abusive relationship when he encouraged her to have what she understood would be bereavement counselling with him. This relationship continued for four years until he left the organisation and it had lasting consequences. As the 'counselling' progressed, McBride (1999, 11) discussed her concerns about Jim's increasingly sexualised behaviour with her spiritual director, a priest. His response was that it was 'the woman's job to keep the relationship on the rails'.

The church's response

As with Dean's experience of McCullough, McBride's of Jim is also very reminiscent of my own experiences of clergy misconduct, with consistent and uncannily similar patterns of grooming, coercion, sexualised, and abusive behaviour. Like Deans and the other women who made formal complaints about McCullough, the proceedings McBride engaged in with the Methodist Church in 1993 were complicated and hampered by a lack of established policy and procedure (McBride 1999, 31). Just as the Anglican Church attempted to evade responsibility for McCullough by claiming that this lay with the university college of which he was principal, and despite the fact that the bishop was chair of the college board (Deans 2001, 66–67, 181), the Methodist Church initially attributed responsibility for Jim to the chaplaincy organisation on the basis that he was employed by them when the abuse occurred (McBride 1999, 49). In my case in the UK, the bishop simply said that the priest was no longer his responsibility as he had left the diocese.

McBride eventually reached a mediated agreement with Jim and, like many women who raise formal concerns about their harassers, soon found herself without a job. The chaplaincy organisation denied any responsibility for sexual harassment by its director and the personal grievance process McBride subsequently underwent with them was aggressive and deeply retraumatising, as the organisation attempted a character assassination (pp. 52–55). Additionally, McBride was subjected to a strict confidentiality agreement that severely limited the support she could access for her ongoing distress at the situation. Non-disclosure clauses are common in sexual harassment settlements, while in cases where settlements are not reached, victims may be threatened with litigation if they speak out.

The repercussions for women involved in the McCullough case were also significant and lasting. One of the Anglican priests interviewed by Sandra Coney for the *Dominion Sunday Times* in conjunction with McCullough had been 'so upset by harassment from male clergy during her training', she considered abandoning her vocation altogether (Coney 24 September 1989 cited in Deans 2001, 57). Deans (2001, 179–180) details the detrimental effects on the careers and vocations of four other women who brought the complaint against McCullough and on four clergywomen who supported them, including Patricia Allan, who lost her job and was made unemployable in the diocese, eventually transferring to ministry in the Methodist Church.[14] Deans was forced out of her role as a non-stipendiary priest and was to spend ten years away from the church. She had to fight to regain her license and initially was made to reapply for it on an annual basis; this requirement is usually triennial (Abuse in Care 2020a(i), 695).

Three more women eventually came forward with official complaints about Jim spanning some 25 years and the Methodist Church had to instigate disciplinary procedures, particularly as three of the survivors had met each other by this time. Both the process and the outcome were unsatisfactory, with Jim himself selecting two of the five-person disciplinary panel. He was, at the time, minister in a joint Anglican/Methodist parish. The outcome was that Jim offered to retire seven months earlier than he had planned, with permission to still be able to celebrate weddings for his immediate family. He was required to undergo counselling. McBride later discovered that Jim was again working in a pastoral role in the Anglican Church. From enquiries she made, it appeared that the Methodist Church had not alerted the Anglican Church to his behaviour, nor had the Anglican church undertaken adequate safeguarding checks.[15]

McBride noted (p. 73) that the Methodist Church had looked after Jim's interests 'very effectively' during the five years since her first complaint, yet there had been no attempt to address the needs of Jim's victims or to institute any kind of redress. Three of the four complaints that were addressed at this point were also related to the chaplaincy organisation, yet the Methodist Church refused to engage in discussion with that organisation. McBride (p. 76) notes the irony of this outcome in a church 'for whom involvement in social justice issues has traditionally been of prime importance'. She does however acknowledge (p. 77) a benefit of the disciplinary process: for the first time in nearly ten years, she had been able to tell her story in its entirety and have it believed.

Jim himself finally brought a hint of his abusive behaviour to public attention when he attempted to sue his church for the disciplinary action it had taken in response to the four complaints (pp. 1, 94). These proceedings were notable not only for Jim making the matter public to some degree (the details of the disciplinary action were not disclosed), but because the Employment Court ruled that as a clergyman Jim was employed by God, not the church and therefore the church could not be sued for his dismissal. McBride was to learn of more women who had been abused by Jim, making seven in total, that she was aware of (p. 97).

Vocation and vulnerability

Recently widowed and newly a working single parent, McBride had been understandably vulnerable, at that point in time, to grooming by Jim who offered her support after the death of her husband. Speaking of her chaplaincy work, McBride (p. 7) comments: 'Given that my own Catholic Church does not ordain women, it was a blessing and delight to be there with a formal ministry role'. Prior to this, McBride had been engaged in ministry in her parish church. She comments:

> The abuse, and what I learned about power structures and power imbalances and the brotherhood of clergy defending each other really put me off hierarchical structures. In terms of ministry, I was a workplace chaplain for seven years while the abuse happened and while I tried to survive the processes. As part of that I trained as a spiritual director. After leaving that organisation, while I was busy trying to recover, I did my counselling training, because I was so committed to working safely with people, as distinct from what had happened to me. In 1999 after a disagreement with the Catholic hierarchy I cut my ties with the Catholic Church. But I'd already been attending the Quakers because I'd found I was going home from Mass every Sunday with a headache from all the male God language. So, from 1996, I worshipped where they didn't talk, with the Quakers.

McBride now describes herself as a post-denominational Christian, having 'had it up to here' with the hierarchies of the Methodist, Catholic, Anglican, and Presbyterian Churches. Like Deans and myself, she also left the church for a number of years. She currently attends a progressive Presbyterian church, but chooses not to officially join that denomination, saying 'it distresses me hugely when the church rules take priority over the gospel. I call that "ecclesiolatry", and I don't want a bar of it'. She has retired from her work as a spiritual director and counsellor, and continues to write, to participate in interfaith events, and to advocate for survivors of clergy abuse. She comments:

> One of my ongoing issues with the Catholic Church is that they preach social justice, they have excellent social justice analysis, and then they don't do it internally for women, or for Rainbow people. I have a nil tolerance for blatant inconsistency. The impact on my spiritual life? God is bigger, wider, and deeper than the church, than Christianity. A vocation to work in the church? I don't know. It was a vocation to ministry for sure. While I may have no ministry *in* the church, there is a strong sense of ministry *to* the church, wounded as it is by patriarchy and clericalism. As an outsider administratively, I can challenge thinking and process from a gospel perspective – which may or may not be heeded. How do I feel about the church now? I've had the lot of them. And it's a great pity that it is like that, because they undermine themselves when they are trying to convince people that this is a good, safe place where you will be looked after and helped to grow. They all have this really good self-image of 'this is what we are, and this is what we do, and this is going to be good for you', and then people get damaged, and people leave and maybe don't darken the door again. How is that helpful? How is that fulfilling their mission to bring people to the experience of God's love?

In making her statement in December 2020 to the Royal Commission of Inquiry into Abuse in Care, the remit of which included 'vulnerable adults' in state and faith-based institutions, Deans outlined the reasons she was vulnerable at the time of McCullough's alleged abuse and why she therefore falls within the terms of reference of the Commission.[16] It is important to note that women experiencing clergy abuse are often vulnerable at that particular point in time in ways they would not usually be, and this vulnerability is often the reason they seek, or are offered clergy support. Such vulnerability is frequently due to a pastoral issue, but it is also implicit in training or educational roles as Deans discovered. That this dynamic is fundamentally structural has been reinforced by #MeToo. Men in powerful positions over women's careers too often exploit that power, positioning themselves as entitled rather than responsible. The relative roles of pastor/teacher/mentor and congregant/student/mentee themselves make women vulnerable. Once clergy overstep professional boundaries, that vulnerability is grossly heightened.

Deans was vulnerable, she notes, because she was training for something *she really wanted to do* (emphasis mine) and her options at that time, as a married woman with young children, called to serve the church in rural Canterbury were limited. She was expected, as an ordinand, to 'put herself into the hands of her tutor'. She was told, bizarrely, to refer to him as 'uncle' which established 'an almost incestuous dynamic'.[17] Her choices, once the abuse began, were 'to leave or stay'. Naturally, Deans was reluctant to compromise her vocation and was realistically concerned that if she reported the abuse, she would not be ordained. (Abuse in Care 2020a(i), 684–685). Instead, she asked to change tutors and was told this was not an option. On top of this, Deans was clearly being psychologically and emotionally manipulated by a sexual predator and increasingly, forced into a situation of secrecy. When she eventually made a complaint, Deans was told that the matter 'was now subject to church law, not secular law' (ibid. 685). This prevented her having access to appropriate criminal proceedings, thereby potentially increasing her vulnerability.

It is perhaps difficult in the largely secular world of 2021 to understand the weight of church authority for New Zealand churchgoers in the 1980s. Equally, in a province where women have been ordained for nearly 45 years (many New Zealand Anglicans today have only known the church with women clergy) the precarious position of women with vocations to ordination at that time may be difficult to grasp. Having said that, since beginning work on this book, a number of women – and men – currently in training have commented on the vulnerability attached to their vocations. We take our vocations seriously and they run deep, being fundamental to our faith and identities. Those responsible for vocational discernment and training have an extraordinary, and at times, arbitrary degree of power over whether we are ordained at the end of that process, or not. I have watched ordinands struggling with issues far less controversial than those I am outlining, who feel unable to discuss them with diocesan or college staff for fear of compromising their vocations.

One common characteristic in the unboundaried clergy I encountered was their enthusiastic support for my vocation, and for women's ordination generally. In an environment where this was still a contentious issue, including within my family of origin, that support was particularly valued and in hindsight, increased my vulnerability to clergy abuse. In a difficult and at times hostile environment, those clergy appeared trustworthy and a safe haven. Ironically, these seemingly supportive relationships proved confusing, distracting, and ultimately deeply damaging to my vocation, my life in the church, and my well-being. As I re-enter the world of theological study and ministry formation, as my academic and spiritual passion reignites, I am reminded of how much I lost when I put my vocation aside nearly 20 years ago, believing that was the only way to keep myself from further harm.

Dr Rocío Figueroa, a theologian and lecturer at Te Kupenga Catholic Theological College, was introduced to the influential Catholic lay order, Sodalitium Christianae Vitae, in Peru in 1983, and was one of five young women to set up a women's branch of the community, the Marian Community of Reconciliation (MCR), in 1986. From a young age she had experienced a call to the religious life. At 15, she was sexually abused by her spiritual director, German Doig, Vicar General of the order. Figueroa progressed to become the superior of MCR, but when she challenged the male leadership, she was sent to the community house in Rome, where she worked at the Vatican. It was many years before she was able to fully understand the effects of the abuse, including the psychological and spiritual manipulation she had experienced by the order's male leadership. Figueroa left the order in 2012, having exposed wider abuse by Doig, and by Sodalitium's founder, Luis Fernando Figari.[18] She returned to Peru, where she met her husband, a New Zealander. Here she talks of the effects on her vocation:

I left the community because I had to. I could not stay in a community that was corrupt. I felt disillusioned. I did not want any link with the church, or any community, so I never considered going to another community or congregation. I was absolutely disillusioned with the institution. It wasn't just the response of the community, it was the terrible response from the church.

When I first left the community, I had a profound crisis regarding my vocation, and I thought that everything was a lie. I doubted myself and considered that everything was my invention and that I, in a very naive and stupid way, had been convinced by the members of the community to join them. I thought that I had been manipulated.

As the years passed, I rediscovered myself and my vocation. I realised that it was not a lie, it was an authentic vocation. Since I was a kid, before joining the community, I had wanted to be a nun. I loved Jesus and I wanted to be a consecrated woman.

I no longer think it was a lie – it was a real calling to serve God. I eventually realised that the vocation is inside me, and I continue now serving God with all my heart. But it took me many years to heal that delusion, the idea that I had invented everything and that everything was a lie.

What contributed to the healing?

First, grace. Then I think that I was very patient. I didn't try to force myself. I knew that I needed time to leave the topic of my relationship with God, my vocation, my faith, a little bit away from me. So, I had two years when I didn't think too much about those topics. I tried to have a little bit of distance. It was not about ideas, it was my heart that was wounded and needed to be healed, so first I needed time.

It was interesting. For example, the first year after leaving the community, although I was a theologian, I decided not to teach theology and I began teaching anthropology at the university. I said to myself, 'I will not teach theology, because now I am confused regarding everything: myself and God; my calling and my relationship with him'. I didn't know what was true and what was not, and I needed to process everything again.

I had experienced not only sexual abuse, but also spiritual abuse. I had been manipulated regarding the gospel and theology, so I needed to question my faith and review it and find new categories. I gave myself time to recover without forcing myself. I think it was good. I was patient with myself. And then little by little I began facing different topics. I began asking, 'who is God for me? Who is Jesus? What's the core of his message?'

I had to distinguish between the manipulative elements from the leaders of the community and the real authentic elements from the gospel, reviewing my faith and assuming new categories and approaches. This process has taken me years and I no longer feel that I am manipulated. Everything that I believe has gone through the lenses of my own critical thought, decision and will. So, it has taken me all these years, but I think I have gotten there. What I feel, what I think, is what I really feel and think, and no one has imposed it on me.

Many factors have helped me: patience in the process, the presence of others, trying to heal my heart, then time to question and face all the topics of my faith and reframe them, but also being at peace with it. Before, I was full of anger, and that anger was important. I think it is important to be free and express the anger. I had a time where I expressed my anger and I had loving people who helped me. My husband was always open to listen to me. I let the anger out and that is why now I feel peace.

Finally, for me, it was important to forgive the ones who had damaged me. I don't try to be friends with them at all, but I forgave them. I don't feel any negative feelings towards them. Everything is a big process, of prayer, of being helped by others and also psychological therapy. And, I think, time. You need time to heal.

At the beginning I didn't go to Mass and I was really upset with the institution. But of course, the church is more than an institution, it's a community, and I think during this process I have found many people who are very nice. Also, I received the tradition from my family, from my parents, who were very good people. Why should I renounce or resign from something that belongs to my tradition, to my family, that is in my innermost self, because of some bad people? Yes, there are many aspects of the church that I do not agree with, but it's like any institution; we are human. I don't think that I would be happier in another. For me, it's important to continue in the tradition of my parents. It's part of my identity.

Has going back into theology and theological education been important for you in that healing process?

Absolutely. Because you face your faith again. I questioned my faith. Now I feel that my faith is mature. It was important to discern. Also, working for victims has been empowering. It is important to accept what has happened to you, but also it is fundamental to find a purpose, a meaning for what you have gone through. I try to be a voice for victims, for those who have no voice. For me it has been a path of empowerment and meaning and sense. This helps in the path of healing.

How would you describe your vocation now?

I feel I have been called by God, called by my name to serve him and to love him and to help others and to serve others. Since I was a kid, I had this call, this feeling of being chosen by God to be his instrument, and for me it's very clear. I just want to be his instrument in this world and serve him and serve others. I feel that the way I am living my vocation has changed, but the essence is the same. I belong to him and I am his. That's the core of my vocation.

Do you think you would have left the order if you hadn't been abused?

There were other types of abuse, it was not just sexual. There was spiritual abuse and psychological abuse, so I think I would have left even without the sexual abuse. In my community 150 women left, but very few of them were sexually abused. Many people left because of the other abuses that happened there. I remember growing up I was more and more upset about the misogynist attitude, the way they treated the women, the clericalism. I think I would have rebelled and left in the end, because of the other types of abuse.

Sexual abuse does not happen in a vacuum. Other factors combine to facilitate it. The founders and leaders of Sodalitium were misogynist, manipulative, and abusive, undermining the young women who joined the order, and exploiting them by tasking them to work for the order without remuneration. Figueroa identifies misogyny, abuse of leadership, misunderstanding of obedience, and clericalism as factors that contribute to the spiritual abuse that underpins sexual abuse in the church. As she observes, '[i]f you put clericalism, sexism, and the situation of women together, it's like a bomb' (CathNews New Zealand, 2020). In the following chapter, I examine these factors as they contribute to abuse in the Anglican Church in Aotearoa New Zealand.

Notes

1 Hepburn starred in the 1959 film 'The Nun's Story' based on Kathryn Hulme's novel of that name.
2 In 1970 the Diocese of Waiapu introduced the Admission to Holy Communion of baptised children over eight, the practice was extended to other dioceses following General Synod in 1972.
3 In 1989 there were 120 ordained Anglican women in New Zealand including retired clergy (Neave, 1990, iii). Many of these women were in non-stipendiary and/or part time positions. Of 83 ordained women who responded to a questionnaire in 1989, one was under 30, 14 were aged 30–39 and 16 were single (ibid. 4/3–4/4).
4 Deans does not name McCullough, calling him 'The Reverend Canon R', however he was named in relation to this case in media reports and in evidence to the Royal Commission. Bishop Peter Carrell, for example, outlines the case in his statement to the Commission (Abuse in Care 2021a, 16–18). According to Deans (Abuse in Care 2020a (i), 701), McCullough's response to the allegations was to vilify the women, claiming that they had thrown themselves at him. The women lodged a Title D complaint with the church, which the bishop declined to proceed with, however McCullough's roles in the church were curtailed. The women then made a complaint to the university college of which McCullough was principal, resulting in McCullough's resignation from that role. In subsequent discussion with church leaders, Deans notes that the archbishop told the women that, as clergy, they did not have recourse to civil law and that church law required them to forgive and reconcile with McCullough. The women asked for an apology from McCullough but did not get one. The

church eventually issued an apology and made a financial settlement to nine women (ibid. 702–713, 717–718).

5 See Stephens (2013, 27–29) on creating unhealthy precedents.

6 The names 'Jane' and 'Richard' are pseudonyms.

7 A small town in the North Island's Manawatu District.

8 The Māori Anglican Church, also called Te Hāhi Mihingare.

9 I reflect on this time in Chapter 3.

10 *Exposed: The Church's Darkest Secret*, BBC 2020.

11 Carey resigned from his post as Honorary Assistant Bishop of Oxford in 2017 over his complicity in Ball's abuse and in June 2020 his permission to officiate as a priest was revoked while his involvement in the case of alleged serial abuser John Smyth was investigated (BBC News 2017, 2020).

12 See Kennedy (2013, 27–28) on the importance of naming abuse correctly.

13 Bishop of Christchurch Peter Carrell (Abuse in Care 2021a(i), 2:5) states that records of 'at least thirteen reports of abuse' in that diocese were found prior to the Royal Commission. These did not include the McCullough case as 'the individuals abused by Mr McCullough were adults without any known physical or intellectual vulnerabilities'. In para. 6 he attributes the paucity of records to the diocese's 'poor record keeping'.

14 See Allan's (1996, 32–36) account of this experience.

15 McCullough moved to a job at a private college for overseas students (Deans 2001, 72, 127).

16 The Commission recognises 'the general vulnerability of a person who is under the responsibility of another person or entity', acknowledging that vulnerability 'may also arise in relation to a person's nationality; race; ethnicity; religious belief; age; gender; gender identity; sexual orientation; or physical, intellectual, disability, or mental health status' (Abuse in Care 2018, 7:13).

17 Having said this, the fetishism in some grooming/abuse strategies can be bizarre. I once found a priest kneeling on the floor behind me trying to get under my skirt. Deans and other women who alleged they had been abused by McCullough noted that he had a propensity for exposing himself in churches and public places, a practice the archbishop at the time did not appear to view as problematic (Deans 2001, 95; Abuse in Care 2020a, 41–42). Tom Walker, a Church of England priest, was alleged to have harassed Jo Kind, who worked as his PA from 1989 to 1991, by working naked, ostensibly on the advice of his doctor, and walking around the office in various states of arousal. Walker was 'rebuked' by a disciplinary process in 2015 and Kind was awarded £40,000 after taking civil action (Collins 2019, 16).

18 Figari was finally investigated by the Vatican in 2015 and removed from the order. The new leadership of the order undertook a further investigation in 2017. While the order and the Vatican recognise the legitimacy of the allegations, Figari cannot be prosecuted due to a statute of limitations as the abuse is historic. Figari, Doig (who died in 2001) and three other named leaders were also investigated for child abuse in Peru in 2017 (CNA 2017). The allegations against the leaders of Sodalicio are outlined by Alvear and Tombs (2019, 157–159).

3   #ChurchToo

The Anglican Church in 1980s Aotearoa New Zealand

In this chapter, I return to my own journey in the Anglican Church in New Zealand, exploring my experience as a young woman with a religious vocation in the context of both New Zealand's social history and the shared experience of other women who sought ordination in the 1970s, 1980s, and 1990s.

When I began training for ordination in 1987, many women were crying out for language that acknowledged their presence, respected, and represented them; for language that reflected women's experience of the world and of God. Women were weary of feeling invisible as the church prayed for 'all men' and for its 'brethren' (both terms I have encountered in church services recently) and frankly, God the Father just did not cut the mustard for many of us. We sought to broaden the church's language and imagery to include more feminine and non-anthropomorphised images for God, and to acknowledge all God's people. Not to take out male language altogether, simply to bring balance to a very one-sided affair. 'Male and female God created them', but half of 'them' were missing.

In July 1989, Anglican laywoman Rosemary Neave preached a sermon in which she described seeing a woman in tears after a church service. The woman said that she 'couldn't stand it any longer – the male language roared at her every week from the hymns and liturgy. She left the church'. She was, Neave says, 'a strong, educated, articulate woman and committed Christian'. What was the church becoming if such women could not find a home there? (Neave 1991, 30).

Many women at that time followed theologian Mary Daly, moving 'beyond God the Father',[1] and out of the church altogether. According to Laurie Guy (2011, 428), the number of New Zealand's churchwomen who voted with their feet over the years is unquantifiable. While Guy

DOI: 10.4324/9781003164937-3

suggests that the exodus may have been 'limited to middle-class in-tellectuals', Anglican priest Diane Miller-Keeley (cited by Guy 2011, 428) asserted that women left in droves. At any rate, we now have the answer to Neave's question about what the church was becoming, as dwindling attendance figures bear witness. For so many, the church has become irrelevant, because it has continued to drag its heels on human rights issues, including gender equality and LGBTQ+ rights,[2] and on reforming discriminatory language, which is used to shape and perpetuate inequalities of all sorts.

In the late 1980s, we took our lives in our hands (metaphorically speaking) and used words like 'Mother' to address God in worship. The consequences were often grim. Neave (1991, 30) commented that she could think of few parishes where it would be safe to pray occa-sionally to God as Mother. Even changing the words of hymns to make them inclusive was problematic.

Commenting on the slowness of the church to change despite 20 years of secular feminism, Presbyterian Frances Stuart (1991, 1) won-dered why she and other women still attended church, whether women felt affirmed and spiritually nourished, and whether they were aware of the disparity in the church's message and praxis. She cites Catho-lic theologian Anne Patrick,[3] who described five responses women were making to the church, ranging from unquestioning compliance with patriarchal institutional Christianity to the total rejection of the church and movement into neopagan or post-Christian feminist com-munities. To these, Stuart adds a sixth position, which I particularly identified with: women of liberal theological persuasion who left the church because of the intellectual and spiritual deficit in its teachings and devaluing of women, who have not found an alternative commu-nity and miss having a focus for spiritual expression.

Prior to my decision to leave in 2003, I maintained Patrick's 'Type 5' position – working within the church to transform it, at times meet-ing 'as church' with like-minded women, although such opportunities were few and far between. In choosing one of these positions, Stu-art (1991, 1) says, women are acting as responsible moral agents. It is validating now to hear my attempts then to find my own position of integrity in relation to what ultimately felt like an impossible situation described positively. My failure to comply with the masculinist ideol-ogy and practice of the Anglican Church as a young woman was often (in my experience) seen as troublesome by others and was therefore uncomfortable and painful for me. It was difficult to sustain, and im-possible for me to live without anger and a sense of injustice.

Stuart's discussion focusses on a variety of responses to the patri-archal Judaeo-Christian tradition by some well-known theologians:

Mary Daly, Daphne Hampson, Carol Christ, Judith Plaskow, Rosemary Ruether, and in New Zealand, Susan Adams. She cites Adams' conviction that she 'is church' and that women 'are church' – as much so as men, both ordained and lay (1991, 5). I struggled to have this degree of conviction, always feeling more at home on the fringe, always with a sense that I was battling or intruding when I stepped into the thick of things. As a young woman I was expressing a vocation it often seemed I had no right to – and yet, the conviction of that vocation has not left me. Now, returning to the Anglican Church in Aotearoa New Zealand, I hear the stories of recent converts to the Anglican Church and indeed recent converts to Christianity who are training for ordination, and wonder why in the 1980s, as a life-long Christian and a life-long Anglican, I felt I had so little right to be here.

Adams (1988, 20) noted at that time, that given the androcentric nature of the church, it was unsurprising that many feminist women were considering leaving to establish alternative faith communities. Many in the churches, she states, are acting out of fear in the face of their beliefs being challenged and simply hope that these troublesome women will leave: 'for many traditionalists, feminists have no place in the church' (1988, 20).[4] This issue does not simply affect the churches, however. Adams highlights the influence of traditional male Christian values on New Zealand society and attitudes, asserting that Christian feminists must stay in order to influence social transformation. It is tempting to ponder how much further advanced the churches would be with same-sex marriage and the ordination of committed Christians in same-sex partnerships if those droves of women had stayed.

British theologian Daphne Hampson's 'shattering' decision to leave the church was, Stuart (1991, 2) observes, precipitated by illness following years of frustration, pain, anger, and feelings of worthlessness at the church's denial of her vocation. Eventually she came to interpret the Christian tradition as incompatible with women's equality and adopted a post-Christian position. Banging one's head against the patriarchal brick wall for so long takes its toll on individual women – ultimately to the detriment of the church. Stuart (1991, 3) summarises the common aspects leading to Daly's, Hampson's, and Christ's decisions to leave the church as 'the perception of an extreme threat either to themselves or to women in general, the belief that change is not possible, the belief that they can be more fully human outside the church'. All of those factors influenced my own decision to leave.

How do I feel about those perceptions now?

I left believing that in doing so I was taking myself out of an abusive relationship with the church that would ultimately destroy me. Ironically, with the prospect of ministry in the church no longer available to me (or so I believed), I re-entered an abusive relationship with one of its clergy, with lasting consequences.

As for being more fully human outside the church, how does one assess this? In 2019 I wrote:

> In leaving the church I lost my community and the focus of my creativity. I consciously and deliberately shut down my vocation and my spiritualty. While, over time I have made meaningful connections with people I respect and love, with spiritual traditions I value and feel nurtured by, and have undertaken creative projects that seem to have value for others as well as myself, there is a sense of disjointedness, disconnectedness – of not having arrived, of not being quite whole. I divide my time between different communities in different parts of the world. In my work-life I have my finger in several pies, each of which I love and none of which I feel I give as much attention to as I ought. I have developed a mistrust of organisations, having found they can be equally dysfunctional whether religious or secular. I no longer have a formal or regular spiritual practice – which is not to say I neglect my spiritual life altogether, just that the attention I give it is both spontaneous and sporadic. As an extravert, I do not find it easy to be solitary. The corporate practice of liturgy was my 'way in' to prayer, and its loss the greatest I experienced on leaving the religious life. God has stayed quietly present throughout. I think there is less shame for me outside the church, but for those who are shame-prone, it can arise in any context.

The reactions of women who leave the church, Stuart notes (p. 3), include anger, sadness, a sense of betrayal, regret, 'a joyous move towards a positive and satisfying alternative', or a 'void'. Having moved through most of those stages, I learned to live with the void.

Stuart speaks to the validity of both paths – staying and going. She concludes, however, that while she agrees with those who have left that the church has been a problem for women, she also believes it can provide the solution – provided women stay and work for its transformation (pp. 5–6). She acknowledges that this is not an easy path and advocates the need for women to support each other, suggesting that should this transformation not prove possible in the long run 'the Women Church' will eventually flourish as a permanent separate entity away from the mainline churches'. Some Christian feminists were optimistic in the eighties and early nineties!

Women Church

This was the position also advocated by Rosemary Radford Ruether in her book *Women Church* (1985). Ruether was one of a number of authors whose work was central to the emerging Christian feminism of that decade. This classic Christian feminist text balances a critical hermeneutic of patriarchal Western Christianity with the interim possibility of 'Women Church', leading ultimately to an authentic redemptive community of women and men free from patriarchal constraints. Ruether's book provides a structural analysis of institutional Christianity that I wish I had accessed when I was a young woman training for ordination. In hindsight, an awareness of Ruether's analysis would have made me canny to the dynamics of sexism and coercion I was then grappling with.

As I now read the accounts of women my generation and older, I realise I was not alone in feeling isolated, marginalised, excluded. In 1980, Jo Pelly, at that time married to the warden at St John's College, wrote an article about life there for women, observing that the material resources of the college and the spiritual task of 'self-actualisation' were largely reserved for men. Gender roles remained largely traditional, with women doing the practical work of child-rearing while men did the spiritual work. Each of the ten male staff, she noted, had a wife 'who fries his chops and washes his pants for him' (1980, 5). Of the three women students at the college in 1980, only one 'survived intact', and she did not return for her final year (ibid. 4). This was the nature of Anglican theological training seven years before I started at St John's.

Change across the wider church also proved difficult. As late as 2000, women meeting as church at St Peter's, Willis Street in Wellington were expelled from that community – not as individual worshippers, but as the collective EXperimental ALTernative worship community 'ExAlt', who had organised monthly services at St Peter's for women and men of any religious tradition or none since 1993.[5] Some of those women had been active in the life and ministry of that congregation for many years. Services were structured around themes ranging from the changing of the seasons to Te Tiriti o Waitangi,[6] peace, or reinterpretation of biblical narratives. Some were gentle and reflective, others more 'challenging and uncomfortable' as arguably, they ought to have been; there is nothing comfortable about the ministry and gospel of Jesus.

In August 2000, in response to media coverage of professional misconduct, the ExAlt service focussed on the issue of surviving clergy abuse. Women present, including some who had suffered clergy abuse, found the service helpful and healing, however, the male vicar viewed it as 'hostile to the church' and lacking resolution. Supported by a group of conservative women on the vestry, the vicar of St Peter's, a church whose signage proclaimed, 'the Open Door welcomes you', expelled ExAlt and with it, a diverse group of women committed to engaging in the serious exploration of Christianity.

The 'lessons' learned by the ExAlt faith community and onlookers were summarised by Pat Booth (Booth et al. 2001, 19). She noted the unacceptability of confronting the issue of abuse within a public church service, the failure of conservative women to support those working to expose gender-based injustice, the church's reticence to engage in dialogue with others in the local community while imposing its own perspective, and that the 'open door' is only for those who fit in.

Judith Dale (Booth et al. 2001, 20) adds to this a broader, contextual assessment of the times, describing the resurgence of a moral conservatism:

> There has been a feeble liberal Christian presence in Aotearoa New Zealand for some time, as the growth of the moral right and various other manifestations of backlash replace the liberatory explorations of the 70s, 80s and early 90s. Instead, now, there is a hunkering down, a consolidation, a closing of ranks; and, of course, in world terms, this is true economically and politically.

The loss of a feminist voice at the fringe of the church was, Dale points out (ibid.) by no means unusual.

Such groups, meeting within or without church spaces provided women with 'education, support, consciousness-raising and ritual, in a genuine experiment with a new form of feminist religious life and commitment' (Lovell-Smith 1993, 189), offering the context for meaningful relationships and support that is so essential for women's well-being,[7] and a space for women to engage theologically and spiritually in discussion and ritual as they moved away from institutional Christianity. Describing the 'Wellington Christian Feminists' group, which met from 1977–1990, Lovell-Smith (p. 189) noted that 'for many of the women these meetings replaced the church they had left, as they identified and disowned the patriarchal basis of their faith'. Study of Daly's *Beyond God the Father* was to prompt many of the women to adopt a post-Christian feminist stance. Membership of the group comprised well-educated Pākehā women from a range of religious backgrounds, a number of whom identified as lesbian. Notably, they shared 'a common past of serious, continuing commitment to faith' (ibid.).

Lovell-Smith's description of the membership of the Wellington group would support Guy's assertion that many of those women who left the church in this period were middle class intellectuals and it seems that the loss of these women may have contributed to the church's subsequent stasis on justice and equality issues. The group was committed to educating and learning from other women's groups and to connecting with feminist women who were often isolated in their churches.

The inception of the feminist spirituality journal *Vashti's Voice* in 1978 had enabled women to keep in touch and informed about the national network that evolved as local groups connected. I was 17 at that point, and thoroughly immersed in the patriarchal church, oblivious to the stirrings of feminism going on in the world outside – although beginning to be puzzled by the fact that the outside world did not always appear to be the way it was described to me in the inside world of home, my Anglican girls' secondary school, and church. Looking through those early type-written and hand-illustrated Gestetner-produced copies I can imagine the excitement Janet Crawford (1997, 3) describes as she and fellow editor, Mitzi Nairn, received copy and new subscriptions from women who 'somehow had discovered Vashti and found that they were not alone in their feelings of dis-ease and their struggles with the institutional churches and patriarchal Christianity'. I was not to come across *Vashti's Voice* until the mid-1980s, and even then, I do not think I really connected with it, or with the network of women who wrote and read it, despite knowing a number of them. Judith McKinlay (1997, 3) writes of the aim of *Women's Voice*, a Dunedin-based publication that came out of a sub-group of the 'Women in Church and Society Committee' of the Presbyterian Church, to reach out to women who were isolated in terms of faith and feminism. She describes the 'heady days' of emergent feminist scholarship and the tempering of this excitement by the constant struggle to 'push water uphill' in working for change and for the recognition that women's lives and stories were also valid.

Vashti's Voice ceased production in 1992 and was resurrected in amalgamation with *Women's Voice*, as *Vashti's Voices* in 1997, providing a forum for women's theological reflection on church and broader social issues until 2006. The gap left by the demise of *Vashti's Voices* was not subsequently filled. It is tempting to ask whether the absence of a local Christian feminist theology journal is linked with the flabbiness of responses to feminist concerns in the church currently.

It seems ludicrous to me now to know that like-minded women were certainly out there when I was an ordinand and that they may have been a source of support, yet I had failed to really take advantage of that. But then, I was being offered 'support' that was right on my doorstep and as one is drawn deeper into an abusive relationship, isolation begins to set in. Additionally, those networks were by and large peripheral to the mainstream churches and were certainly not viewed by the churches as a resource. It was far more in the interests of the hierarchy to keep certain women apart. Adams (2015, 18–19) notes the isolation experienced by women seeking ordination in New Zealand in the 1970s: 'There was no sense', she says, 'that I was part of a bigger movement of women challenging the traditions and theology of the church either here in New Zealand or elsewhere in the world'. Women with vocations to the priesthood were out on a limb. Additionally, women who were seeking ordination were seen by some Christian feminists to be conforming to the church's patriarchal structures, and therefore were sometimes kept at arm's length.

As second-wave feminism gave women confidence to work for change in the church as well as secular society, we hoped for transformation in models of ministry, relationship, liturgy, theology, discourse, social justice. Forty years down the track, Adams notes that while there were changes, as Penny Jamieson's episcopal ministry in the 1990s demonstrates, it is debatable whether the feminist vision of an inclusive church has really borne fruit. Feminism, Adams argues (2015, 32–33), is marginal once more, and the church continues to marginalise the LGBTQ+ community by excluding those in committed sexual partnerships from ordained leadership as they once excluded women. The church must move, Adams urges, from the notion of 'inclusivity', which invites people in and subtly invites them to change – to 'become like us' – to an appreciation of diversity, a respectful sharing of perspectives through which difference can be celebrated.

An inclusive church?

According to the McCrindle report *Faith and Belief in New Zealand* (2018, 41–42), the biggest block to Christianity for non-Christians and church-going Christians alike, and particularly for post-baby boom generations, is the church's stance and teaching on homosexuality. This is closely followed by gender inequality. I was not surprised to learn that a former fellow student who was vehemently opposed to women's ordination in the 1980s, now opposes those in same-sex relationships who are seeking ordination or asking the church to bless their relationships. As the church has attempted, albeit feebly, to bring itself into line with broader socio-political advances in the area of same-sex relationships, a number of clergy have led their congregations out of communion with the Anglican Church of Aotearoa New Zealand and into GAFCON;[8] a splinter group that appears to me to be more invested in keeping people out of the church than in spreading a gospel of love and inclusion. This gatekeeping, which misinterprets Christianity as the obligation to judge others rather than to reach out to them, is the product and manifestation of masculinist culture and ultimately is driven by fear.

The Revd Dr Paul Reynolds is a lecturer and researcher at St John's College in Auckland, and a priest in Te Hāhi Mihingare.[9] I sought his reflections on the aspects of the culture of the Anglican Church in Aotearoa New Zealand that facilitate abuse.

There are a number of things. One is gender. It has taken a significant amount of time for women to achieve any recognition within the church, despite New Zealand pioneering women's leadership in some respects. The rest of the world has trailed behind, and that's significant in itself. Not only in the church but also in society more broadly. Women getting the vote, homosexual law reforms and so on. They are all significantly late, but other countries are far later. So, if you take women getting the vote, that was 1893. It was quite early compared to other places. And then Anglican women being ordained priest in 1977 and bishop in 1990. The first Māori woman bishop was only consecrated in 2019.

If you look at the decriminalising of homosexuality, the Homosexual Law Reform Bill was passed in 1986. Yet the Anglican Church has taken thirty-plus years to get to the point of allowing same-sex blessings, not even marriage, just blessings. That sounds easy, but it's not, because there are a whole lot of hurdles that have to be gotten through before you actually get that blessing in an Anglican church. One is that the couple need to be civilly married already. Next, they have to find a priest who is willing to do the blessing, and then they have to get the permission of the bishop. Then there is the question of whether they would be supported by that faith community. So many hurdles are put in place. It seems like it's such a progressive thing that the Anglican Church has done, but actually it's not. It's taken thirty years just to get a same-sex blessing, even though same-sex marriage is legal now.[10] I don't understand what that says about our church. And that's just in New Zealand.

Internationally, I've been absolutely gobsmacked with the antics and behaviour of GAFCON, who are members of our Anglican Communion worldwide. I have to question whether they are in fact Anglican, because they are just so vicious, unkind, and unchristian. That's not a church which I believe is just, right, and good.

Additionally, it takes such a long time for the Anglican Church to approve and decide on anything, such as ordaining women or same-sex blessings in the church, let alone acknowledging that there are LGBTQ+ priests and ministers within the Anglican Church. That's on the downlow.

When you become a priest within the Anglican Church, you are expected to live a moral life. There's an ethical, faith-based model of good conduct. Yet many priests we know personally and also through the history of the Anglican Church have slept around, including bishops. The two-facedness of it smacks me in the face. So, as a priest, that behaviour is an expectation. But my experience is that the behaviour of an LGBTQ+ priest is held at a higher standard than any other. This is just one of many examples of the two-facedness and hypocrisy within the church. Of course, a lot of the LGBTQ+ community who are of faith have left. There are others, like me, who are there because my faith is strong and I do believe in Te Hāhi Mihingare, although that has eroded significantly over the short time I have been in the church.

There's also the diminishing of the role of women in the church. The unacknowledged role of women in the church. That comes through strongly in the relatively small number of women in senior positions and how many are represented on significant church bodies, councils, committees, General Synod, and so on. There are specific criteria for General Synod members from each amorangi or diocese. There are places where there is a requirement that women should be represented, but if you look at all those different bodies overall, women aren't fairly represented. When they are, and when they are given positions of responsibility, I know from experience that their authority, their leadership has been undermined by men. If a woman has been chosen above a man for a role or position, there can be a real resentment and jealousy and antagonism towards that person. Not only directly towards that person, but indirectly through all of the other relationships and networks that they have, to undermine women who have been placed in positions of authority.

A survey of women's representation in church governance by the Anglican Women's Studies Centre in 2016 showed that women were significantly underrepresented on Anglican boards and General Synod committees and commissions, including those concerned with liturgy, doctrine, and social justice (de Pont 2016, 6). Reynolds continues:

> The church is patriarchal – that's obvious, and even though there have been changes, the church still is constrained by its patriarchal lineage and tradition. Notably, that patriarchal dominance and authority is predominantly white, heterosexual, and male, and difference is seen as a challenge to the church. Sexuality, gender, disability, and any other difference is seen as a threat to the order and the stability of the church, of the traditional church.
>
> *Why do you think they are so invested in it? Is it power and status?*
>
> Yes, power and status definitely. If a female has power and status over a male, that's threatening. Alongside that, it's how society is set up generally, just about every institution and everything we practise, even language is male dominated. Our society and cultures within New Zealand are saturated with male dominance. The church isn't alone in these things. Although there is at one level, an acceptance, an openness, and a generosity towards inclusivity within the Anglican Church, when you really get down to it, it's not inclusive. It actually stops people from coming through the door of the church. There doesn't have to be a direct confrontation to say, 'you're not welcome here'. You get the feeling; you get that feeling immediately coming through the door.
>
> There's a whole lot of unwritten stuff around sexuality in the church. There's a higher expectation for LGBTQ+ [and for women] to be in a 'right relationship' and be on best behaviour, and yet, all over the world within the Anglican Church there are heterosexual male priests who have behaved extremely badly. There's a whole other standard for those who are different. Even if you have a disability, not only do you have your disability, but you have to be a better priest than any other priest. There are higher expectations for anyone of difference and yet the benchmark for anyone who is not of difference is low.

'Sarah' has been an Anglican priest for many years. Her experience further illustrates the engagement with social justice that was driven by feminists in the church in the 1980s, which has since fallen away with clearly detrimental results. Additionally, she illustrates Reynolds' observations about the way women in leadership are undermined.

> My story begins when I was a lay person and there were things like the Rob McCullough abuse saga. A group of us women were so

concerned about the way things were going that we formed a group called the WOMB group, Women Organised to Monitor Bishops. We would rock up to the archbishop's office, and he would always see us. As lay women, we were very involved in wanting the church to address sexual abuse particularly, and the gay issue, or rather, the heterosexual issue that beat up gays, that was prominent for us too. A lot of social issues coalesced for us around monitoring our bishops.

Back then was a heyday. The rise of Christian women's voices influenced by the secular women's movement and the women's conferences that we were holding that were supported by the church, as well as men's groups supporting change for women brought a lot of respect. I don't think we've ever been back there. And it seemed that when Penny Jamieson was made bishop, the church went 'right, that's the women's stuff, we've done it, we've achieved it'.

The environment around Penny was so toxic and so bad. There was a strong move to bring a Title D against her because she said things that offended male clergy and she acted on reports of abuse and that was not well received. There were cartoons of her and her husband in the newspaper, there was horrible stuff put in their letterbox, her car was scratched during a service. She was pilloried. Terrible things happened in the liturgy. For example, she processed in at a service and when she got to the bishop's chair there was a note in large black type saying REPENT. And when she went to the altar and opened the prayerbook to begin presiding there was a similar note stuck to the page.

Richardson (2015, 186) also commented that he observed 'a level of personal attack and critique' during Jamieson's time in office that he has not seen since in the province, and which took its toll on Jamieson and her husband. Understandably, Jamieson (1998) herself commented:

I am too ashamed of my church to give public voice to some of the tactics and sick projections that have been used. The continuing subtle, even underground power of patriarchy, whether exercised by men or by women, to wound and destroy from a base of self-righteousness is truly appalling.

As Sarah describes her life in the church now, and the experiences of other ordained women she knows, she gives concrete examples of the exploitation and lack of respect shown to some women clergy by their male colleagues, including examples of women being scapegoated and undermined for applying for positions of leadership. To cite them here would risk identifying those women, however, her observations again echo Reynolds'. Speaking more generally, she comments:

> In all the things that facilitate abuse in any sector, what are the markers? Well, there's vulnerability, and I think vulnerability has increased in the church. I don't really see people with disabilities having any status whatsoever, particularly women. Vulnerability and being different. Ageism is a horrible thing in the church right now. The church would fall down if some of us weren't there taking services. And then thrashing lay women to death. I think the way the church uses women is highly problematic. But definitely vulnerability, difference, and disadvantage. The disadvantaged are doubly disadvantaged in the church.
>
> *How has your experience of this undermining of women affected your sense of vocation and faith?*
>
> My faith isn't dependent on what the church does. It never has been really. I think the downside has been that it has put me in states where I have been angry. It's made me overtly reactive, which hasn't always been helpful. And I think it has meant the side-lining of me in some instances. I don't trust anyone in authority in the church. I have to really force myself to go to the Eucharist on Sundays now. I feel physically sick when I hear accolades from women for 'the poor vicar', because I know he talks about them and the work they do in the most dismissive, disrespectful ways.

As Figueroa highlighted in the previous chapter, sexual abuse is only one aspect of a much broader structural problem. Sarah continues:

> When women who really want to draw attention to problems and encourage positive change do that in the church currently, the pushback is strong; it's diminishing and it's silencing. The church seems to be less of a respecter of persons now than it ever has been. There's been no real assessment of women's ministry or the suffering this undermining of women causes. It's a form of neglect. I see to this day women who are used abusively and forced to speak gratefully. Especially older women clergy, of whom I am one, who are excluded from decision making, are regularly 'called to order', and who have no pathways to speak about it without being construed as pathetic, needy, or wanting power. It would be termed elder abuse in the secular world. From my experience, there are three consistent factors that create the conditions for

abuse: secrecy passing as confidentiality, power passing as leadership, and canonical legalities passing as accountability.

Sarah's experience is disheartening. When I returned to the church in Aotearoa in 2019, I had expected to find an inclusive community where women's ministry was respected and where women were well-represented across the institution. While women's ministry is no longer controversial, there is a deep malaise at the heart of the church.

Language

By the time ExAlt had been expelled from their home at St Peter's in Wellington, I had been away from that church – the faith community that had nurtured my journey in 1985–1986 (and where I had participated in meaningful women-led worship on occasion) for 14 years and had by then established a feminist theology study and worship group in a UK parish. During that time, I often nostalgically cited the progress the church in New Zealand had made in terms of inclusive language and worship, and women's ministry, little realising that, at some point, that progress had evidently come to a halt, or worse had backslidden. Despite the increasing availability of inclusive language resources and the publication in 1989 of *A New Zealand Prayer Book/ He Karakia Mihinare o Aotearoa*, which significantly addressed the issue, Crawford (1997, 4) notes that inclusive language was still not regarded as important in many churches in the late 1990s, and some had actively decided against making changes. Similarly, despite there being increasing numbers of women studying and teaching theology, it was possible to complete a theology degree without engaging with feminist theology (ibid. 4–5). A similar explanation to that suggested by Sarah was given to me: the church was content to congratulate itself on having ordained women – and leave it at that.

Preaching at the 40th anniversary of the ordination of women to the priesthood in Christchurch's Transitional Cathedral in 2017, Patricia Allan (2018, 3) spoke of her sadness that 'we are still, in our worship services, often presented with an all-male God and encouraged to sing hymns that still name us women as men or brothers'. This, despite the issue of inclusive language being raised first at General Synod in 1978.[11]

I discuss the church's language with Archbishop Philip Richardson:
I remember in the 1980s, there was quite a group of strong, vocal women, including myself, who were pushing for inclusive language, but that seems to have vanished.

Yes, it feels like we've gone backwards. I found myself sitting in a large service recently listening to the words of the hymns and thinking, 'I thought we had taken some really clear principled steps to challenge that language'. It was really strong patriarchal, quite chauvinistic language. I was quite shocked. I'm not sure when it all started to sneak back in but it's really prevalent again. When I raise it, it's often the younger cohort of leaders who find it difficult to understand why it's an issue.

How do we address that?

I try to be much more observant. If I'm given a service to proof, an ordination service for example, I try to be really intentional about looking at the language and asking for changes. The simplest thing is to just change it yourself, but you do that and no one other than yourself is aware of it. Something I've noticed is that, when I have raised it and I've offered an alternative, like 'All creatures of our God, rejoice', instead of, 'All creatures of our God and King', people go, 'oh yeah, I get that, and actually that's a lot nicer', so it's not that there's a kind of entrenched opposition.

It seems to me that language is very much the driving factor in how we behave, yet there's still a language and theology that underpins or facilitates abuse and facilitates the lack of women in leadership roles and those kinds of inequalities, and that seems to be something really fundamental that needs to be addressed in order to change things.

Yes, I agree completely. I think those battles that so many women fought in the 80s and early 90s around all of that, we can't afford to allow that to slip through our grasp. We've got to try and retrieve that. An example is around almost a resurgence in the language of submission, and I'm not meaning necessarily the 'wives submit to your husband' type metaphor. If you look at some of the modern worship songs, they have a very, very patriarchal overload in them, and it is all about submission. It might not be specifically inviting women to submit, it's more generic. We, as the people of God, should submit to this patriarchal God. But it is a patriarchal God. You've got patriarchy and all the imagery of the maleness of God talking about how we all need to submit. That translates into propping up what is essentially patriarchy in the church, as I found myself saying in the Royal Commission. I think that remains one of the biggest threats to us. That in spite of having women in leadership, in spite of all of that work that was done, nonetheless, it remains very, very patriarchal and it's supported by the language. Part of me felt that it wasn't a bad thing that it was four male bishops in the witness stand [at the Royal Commission] because we are perpetrators, as a breed. So, it was right and appropriate, but it also sent out another kind of message, which was, 'here's what the leadership of the church looks like; a bunch of opinionated men'.

What I have observed in the 20 years that I've been bishop is the number of disclosures around inappropriate language, things that someone might have said in the past, 'boys will be boys' or, 'it was a bit of harmless flirting'. It's not harmless and it's not flirting. For example, I received a complaint about a priest who had commented on a woman's appearance – a series of comments that were clearly not appropriate. Now, in that case, I held that priest accountable for that use of language.

Can you say what that process involved?

It was a Title D process[12] and it involved us following what the new process requires, which sets the church taking action against the respondent in an almost traditional legal sense, rather than all too often the complainant having to drive the complaint. So, it amounted to a charge sheet in effect, which was 'In the matter of the Diocese of … versus the name of the respondent' and then a list of the things complained about, and where they, in my view, may have breached professional standards. Then the respondent had the opportunity to respond to that, and in fact in that particular case, he recognised the adverse effect his comments had on the complainant and fully took responsibility for that. And we came to a determination in relation to that case, so there was a consequence for the behaviour.

Previously, those kinds of comments would have been regarded as trivial and dismissed.

I was reading a historic case where an allegation was made against a hospital chaplain who, on the pretext of prayer, had placed his hand inside a woman's hospital gown. The response of the bishop of the day was, 'well, boys will be boys', which, if measured against the recent case that I've just described, would now be unusual. I would hope that my response to the recent case would be reasonably typical of the way bishops would now handle similar situations. I certainly hope that we will have that level of consistency from the new Ministry Standards office, because that's exactly why we've established a semi-autonomous body, to get that very consistency. The process has to be transparent, it has to be fair, and it has to be balanced. But it also needs to be clear that if someone discloses that they felt harassed, as was the case in the example I've given, that has to be the starting point – not whether you think the male respondent was simply being a lad.

Constructs like 'boys will be boys' and claims of harmless flirtation play into a broader discourse that facilitates rape culture. These patriarchal constructs include purity culture and complementarianism and are justified within Christianity by appeals to scripture. Purity culture locates sex, particularly for girls and women ('boys will be boys', after all), strictly within the confines of heterosexual marriage and commodifies female bodies by attaching their worth to sexual purity. Complementarianism asserts that men and women have distinct, divinely ordained gendered roles in which women must submit to and support male authority and headship. Complementarianism 'validates gender inequality' and legitimises male control, dominance, and violence, especially towards intimate partners (Blyth 2021, 69).

Purity culture, complementarianism, and the Bible

Dr Emily Colgan is a senior lecturer at Trinity Methodist Theological College, Auckland. We discussed the issues that scaffold abuse in the church.

For quite a while now, I have been concerned by the church's obsession with purity culture. Although on the surface 'purity' sounds fairly innocuous and innocent, it's insidious. And it permeates our congregations to varying degrees. Often when we think of purity culture, we think of extreme American evangelical churches, with purity balls, purity rings, and abstinence pledges, which I don't think are as common in Aotearoa. But the concepts of purity and modesty still play a really strong role in most of our churches. Messages of virginal purity, dressing modestly so as not to tempt people of the opposite sex, saving yourself for God and marriage are still pretty common. Often this can escalate into policing how women (in particular) act and behave. Purity rhetoric establishes gendered interactions that conceive of women as passive and submissive, or as temptresses, while men are active, pursuers, and agents. This rhetoric provides the foundation for abuse to flourish.

Shame is also very central to purity culture – the shame of being associated with impurity – and shame contributes to silence. It contributes to an intricate web of interconnected problems that form the foundation for abuse to flourish. I don't think we in the church are talking about those things. I don't think we're challenging purity culture and modesty culture. What do we teach kids in youth groups? Do we teach them about consent and healthy sexualities and safe sex? Do we teach them about birth control? About queer sexualities? About abusive relationships?

I know that in most churches, even those I would describe as fairly middle of the road or socially progressive, it's still 'well, best not to have sex before marriage', not to be flirty and promiscuous. We see the results of this further down the line when it comes to, 'she asked for it' or 'she tempted him' and so on. All of those classic rape myths: what she was wearing, what she was doing, where she was, all of that comes out of purity culture. 'She must have been doing something wrong'. It's all part and parcel, and I don't think we talk about it in our churches.

One of the added problems in churches is that we have purity culture and rape myths, which are also peddled in everyday secular society, but when we bring them into a church context, it has that additional element of the spiritual realm, so our messages hold extra weight because God is involved. God likes purity, God doesn't like impurity. By fetishising purity, the moral and spiritual worth of girls and women is measured according to their sexual status. Purity messages have an even greater authoritative aspect when we bring in the theological heavyweight stuff. We start seeing problematic theologies develop that further embed these gendered purity messages; theologies around forgiveness, reconciliation, sacrifice, and sin. All of that starts getting wrapped up in the purity discussion as well. So, these purity messages create environments where sexual violence can flourish and then make it very difficult for survivors to name and speak out about this abuse because of the shame associated with it. In addition to this, we also see the church being lethargic in its response, because the first reaction is, 'let's talk about forgiveness' and 'let's talk about reconciliation', and it complicates matters. They're such interconnected issues which reinforce each other, and we need to start talking about this dynamic.

Scripture is frequently used to reinforce both purity culture and rape culture in the church and wider society. The three-volume series *Rape Culture, Gender Violence, and Religion* (Blyth, Colgan, and Edwards 2018) offers perspectives on the intersection of religion, scripture, and rape culture and is a valuable resource to anyone seeking to understand abuse in a religious context. Similarly, several volumes in this Focus Series, not least those by its editors (Blyth 2021, Stiebert 2020), make significant contributions to the discussion on the Bible's role in facilitating rape culture. Presbyterian minister, Ruth Everhart's *The #MeToo Reckoning* (2020), intersperses the narrative of her personal experience of sexual abuse at the hands of a senior clergyman and accounts of other abuse cases in the Presbyterian Church in the US with insightful scripture interpretations that challenge and counter the narratives of rape culture.

By way of an example of the use of scripture to disadvantage women, I include a reflection from my own experience of listening to sermons by male clergy about Jesus' encounter with the Samaritan woman (John 4: 4–42). These have focussed judgementally on the woman's sexuality. The preachers included an elderly Franciscan priest who exclaimed to the community of nuns I belonged to in horrified tones, 'she has had so many husbands she is practically a prostitute'. Sometime into my relationship with the British priest, a repeat abuser who would resort to emotional abuse and sometimes violence if I refused to have sex with him, I sat in the midst of the congregation and listened in disbelief and fury as he announced that the Samaritan woman was 'probably a sex addict'. Time and time again, the real message of that gospel encounter was lost as male clergy opined about the morals of an unfortunate woman who was probably doing her best in a culture where women were dependent on men for their economic survival. The message of the gospel was distorted repeatedly as male clergy enunciated the polarity between a perfect God-man and a 'fallen woman' whose value as a human being was defined solely by sex.

Early last year, I sat in a New Zealand church and held my breath as the congregation watched a dramatisation of the story on video. The characterisation was fascinating. Jesus was drop dead gorgeous, flirtatious, and coy. The woman mature, cautious, analytical, honest. If anyone was sexualised in that encounter, it was Jesus. I waited for the judgement from Jesus. It did not come. The 'you have had five husbands and the man you are living with is not your husband' statement that is usually so damning, was delivered with such subtlety it barely registered. For the very first time, I understood the message. The woman was not confronted, she was astounded. The focus of the story was not a moral diatribe from Jesus about the woman's marital status, but the woman's recognition of Jesus, the Messiah. The point of Jesus' revelation 'you have had five husbands ...' was not to judge the woman, but to help her believe by telling her something he could not possibly have known as a simple human stranger. The woman's immediate response was to recognise Jesus, to summon those around her to Jesus, to bring them to faith. This woman was one of the first evangelists. The people did not shun her, they listened and followed. In a society built on men's exploitation of women, there would have been many like the Samaritan woman. Women struggling to live and rear children in a world where to not have a husband meant poverty and deprivation. For centuries, this woman, chosen by Jesus to announce his Messiahship, has been demeaned by male preachers and reduced to her sexual history in cultures (biblical and Christian) where (oddly), sexual histories are only legitimate for men. Sadly, in the process, the message of the gospel has been overlooked. Instead of focussing on the incarnation, men have focussed on sex and in doing so, have blamed women.

I waited in anticipation for the sermon. Surely, after this breath-taking portrayal of the gospel message, I could expect a different analysis. Predictably, I was disappointed. Once again, this profound story of Jesus' self-revelation and a woman's witness to it was reduced to a disapproving observation about a woman who had apparently had too much sex.

The misuse of scripture has serious consequences. In the conservative evangelical Diocese of Sydney, which still refuses to ordain women, clergy are sacked if they divorce. There are, ostensibly, biblical grounds for this policy, according to Bishop Michael Stead, who cited 1 Timothy 3:5, 'if anyone does not know how to manage his own family, how can he take care of God's church?' to justify the forced resignation of the Revd David Smith, when his marriage broke down. Smith was told to 'get his wife back' or prove that she was the guilty party (Burke 2020). Evidently, a clergyman who cannot control his wife is not fit to run a parish. In 2018, an *ABC News* investigation concluded that there was a disproportionate incidence of domestic violence in conservative Australian churches, due in part to biblically based teaching on male headship and female subordination. The report stated that conservative evangelical men who attend church sporadically are known to be more likely to assault their partners than men of any other religious or non-religious group, and incidences of domestic violence are higher in communities that advocate male authority. Women are often encouraged by churches to remain in abusive marriages, and scripture is used to justify both this and intimate partner violence by men (Baird and Gleeson, 2018).

Conservative evangelical John Smyth QC, leader of the Iwerne evangelical children's camps in the UK, was alleged to have violently abused almost 100 boys in the UK and Africa under the guise of in-stilling spiritual discipline, a practice he justified using the doctrine of penal substitutionary atonement, which understood the violent death of Jesus as a sacrifice to appease an angry God. Smyth was enabled in his abuse by a number of lay and ordained Christians (Harper and Wilson 2019).

Jayme Reaves (2020, 154–155) reminds us that the power of biblical texts to 'build up and also to destroy' lies both in the authority ascribed to scripture and in the community's use of it. Reading scripture responsibly and educating church members accordingly is the first step to increasing public understanding of the biblical foundations of gender violence in the church and is integral to ending the sexual misconduct of church leaders and physical violence against women by their husbands, including clergy.

Clericalism

The Australian, UK, and New Zealand inquiries into church-based abuse have highlighted clericalism – the indiscriminate high regard for the role of pastor or priest – as a causative factor in abuse. Why do clergy have such authority?

According to abuse expert Thomas Doyle (2006), we cannot underestimate the impact of an enduring global entity of such magnitude as the Catholic Church on the lives of Catholics and non-Catholics alike. For many people, Doyle notes (pp. 189–190), the clergy *are* the church. The Church of England's ties with the British establishment produce a similar effect, as the power, influence and privilege of the institution is transferred to the clergy, especially those in senior roles. Doyle (p. 190) describes clericalism as 'the radical misunderstanding' of the role of clergy in the church and in secular society.

Clerical elitism is compounded by the long-held, theologically justified view that the sacramental power of clergy makes them superior to the laity. Clericalism, with its attendant privilege, derives from both patriarchal institutional power and the misconception that clergy are somehow closer to God than the rest of us. Whether clergy appeal to scriptural authority and the maleness of God or their sacramental role in their claim to clerical privilege, the end result is the same. In her evidence to the New Zealand Royal Commission, Jacinda Thompson described priests as 'having an almost supernatural power in the church because ... they're the only ones that can consecrate the bread and wine for Communion'. Thompson saw the priest as 'representing God' (Abuse in Care 2020b, 437, 472).

Clericalism has long been linked with various types of corruption, not least sexual abuse. The serial abuse by Bishop Peter Ball in the UK is a pertinent example. Despite compelling evidence that he was abusing teenage boys, Ball was supported by senior establishment figures including the Prince of Wales, the Archbishop of Canterbury, and a senior member of the judiciary (IICSA 2019b).[13] Chair of IICSA Alexis Jay observed that the public support Ball received reflected the church's culture at the time (IICSA 2019a). Such support was, she notes, rarely extended to his victims. Suggesting that this culture of clericalism in the Anglican Church in Australia impeded a proper response from church leaders and discouraged the reporting of abuse, the Australian Royal Commission advocated 'greater transparency and a more extensive role for women in both ordained ministry and lay leadership positions' as a remedy.[14]

Clericalism is a mechanism in the maintenance of patriarchy. This is strongly highlighted in the ongoing resistance to women's leadership, for example, in those evangelical churches that do not allow women pastors, and in the Catholic Church which still does not ordain women.[15] This resistance has often been taken to irrational extremes. In the Anglican Church, for instance, there was a legal challenge and a bomb threat at the ordination of the first women as deacons in Australia in 1986 and a protest when the first women were priested in Melbourne in 1992 (Porter 2015). In the debate about women's ordination in the Church of England in the early 1990s, a priest asserted '[y]ou can no more ordain a woman than you can ordain a pork pie' (Rees 2019, 137). In Aotearoa in the early 2000s, a kaumātua (Māori elder) deliberately knocked the consecrated wafers out of a priest's hand as she was administering Communion (Quince 2018, 6).

In 1995, then Archbishop of New Zealand Brian Davis (p. 76) commented that 'the expectation that the ordination of women would lead to radical changes in the decision-making processes, bring new theological perceptions and provide a more nurturing emphasis in pastoral ministry, has not been realised in any dramatic way'. Tragically, it appears that Davis was right. Paradoxically, Paula Gooder (2015) highlights the *increasing* clericalisation of the Church of England *as consequent to* the legislative process around women's admission to the orders of deacon, priest and bishop as that church debated whether each distinct order could be available to women. Notably, in seeking to preserve a broad church, the Church of England encouraged 'an ongoing attitude of hostility towards the ministry not only of ordained women, but also of men ordained alongside them' (p. 67). It is tempting to wonder what the church would look like now had such provision not been made – and to consider the implications for the Anglican Church in Aotearoa New Zealand, which has made similar provision in respect of its fair dealing (or not!) with the LGBTQ+ community.

In 1985, Ruether identified the necessity to dismantle clericalism in order to liberate the church from patriarchy. Ironically, it seems that women's ordination has further reinforced this model. Rather than changing the system, lay women have been side-lined by it and clergy-women have been subsumed by it (Slee 2015). Perhaps Ruether (1985, 60) was right: the only way for the church to change in any radical way was for women to withdraw and 'collectivize their own experience and form a critical counterculture to patriarchy', before ultimately re-uniting with those who are not willing to be bound by the constraints of masculinist culture. Ruether's argument for this was that women 'have lacked a critical culture of their own' (p. 59). Clearly this has changed significantly, however, a recurring theme in discussions I had two years ago with several women about their experience in theologi-cal training in Aotearoa New Zealand was their sense of isolation, and a mistrust of women in other Tikanga and women within the church's hierarchy, when it comes to sharing deeply. Additionally, the violent backlash against feminism globally necessitates a renewed commit-ment to address gender concerns, including within the church.

Unless those in church governance are willing to boldly instigate some key changes regarding language, justice, and equity and to model respectful leadership, abuse in the church will not change.

Notes

1 Mary Daly (1928–2010) was a radical feminist philosopher and author of the seminal text *Beyond God the Father* (1973).
2 Lesbian, gay, bisexual, transgender, queer, and other sexual identities.
3 Patrick, Anne (1989) 'Women and Church – Reconsidering the Relation-ship' in *Miriam's Song III* cited in Stuart (1991).
4 This attitude persists in churches. A recent social media post claimed that feminism is against the family unit, divisive, 'hateful', and against God's will and plan.
5 Booth et al. (2001) 18–23.
6 The Treaty of Waitangi, New Zealand's founding document, which was signed at Waitangi in the Bay of Islands in 1840.
7 Jordan, Walker, and Hartling (2004) highlight the importance of mutual sharing and support for women's mental health.
8 GAFCON 'Global Anglican Future Conference' began meeting in 2008 in reaction to the consecration of an openly gay bishop, Gene Robinson, in the USA in 2003 and the subsequent blessings of same-sex unions in some provinces of the Anglican Church.
9 The Māori Anglican Church, which dates from the adoption of the gospel by Māori at Oihi Bay in 1814 and comprises five amorangi (dioceses).
10 Same-sex marriage has been legal in New Zealand since 2013.
11 The motion was drawn up by Janet Crawford (Crawford 2018, 3–4).
12 The Ministry Standards canons of the Anglican Church in Aotearoa, New Zealand, and Polynesia, revised in 2020, which includes the disciplinary process.

13 The actions of these men, their responses, and the church's embarrassment at its failings are summarised in the introduction to IICSA's (2019b) investigation report and detailed in the body of the report (see, for example, pp. v–vi, 133–136, 171–174).

14 See 'Anglican Church' at https://www.childabuseroyalcommission.gov.au/religious-institutions [accessed 31.5.2021].

15 See Crary (2021) for a discussion of leadership and abuse in the Southern Baptist Convention.

4   #WhereTo?

Negative perceptions

'Church abuse has the greatest negative influence on [New Zealanders'] perceptions of Christians and Christianity', with 76% of respondents citing it as having a significant negative influence (McCrindle 2018, 42). Clearly abuse must be addressed if the church is to regain credibility in an increasingly secular society. Appeals to Christian principles of care, compassion, and integrity in the church's approach to abuse within its walls have too often fallen on deaf ears, and wider public accountability may prove necessary if change is to happen. As well as being essential to safeguarding, revising its response to sexual and other forms of abuse is crucial to the church's survival.

The churches represented in the Royal Commission of Inquiry into Abuse in Care, the Salvation Army, the Anglican Church, and the Catholic Church, emphasised the importance of rigorous discernment, psychological and police screening, and boundaries training in their selection and training of candidates for ministry. The Royal Commission has prompted these institutions to reconsider their responses to survivors from survivor-focussed and trauma-informed approaches and to adopt transparency, accountability and consistency in their policies and procedures. This Commission is still in process and its overall influence on church practice will not be evident for some time. It is to be hoped that those churches that participated will have learned some valuable lessons, not least, from listening to the experiences of the survivors who courageously came forward, and from being involved in a more honest and respectful process than they themselves have often delivered.

The focus of this volume has been twofold: to describe the experience of clergy sexual misconduct by women whose lives and vocations to Christian ministry and church leadership have been affected by it,

DOI: 10.4324/9781003164937-4

and to examine some of the systemic sociocultural and religious factors that allow clergy sexual abuse to thrive.

In Chapter 2: #MeToo, I set out the story of my vocation and the professional misconduct of several male clergy that impeded it. I also considered the stories that other survivors of clergy abuse have so generously shared with me and for a wider readership, using our various experiences to illustrate the common patterns and themes of clergy abuse.

In Chapter 3: #ChurchToo, I described the culture that has facilitated sexual abuse by church leaders, beginning with the setting in which I first experienced clergy misconduct, the Anglican Church in Aotearoa New Zealand in the 1980s. Various themes emerged in this chapter: the alienation of many women through language that excludes us and does not represent our experience; the easy slippage from language that privileges men and renders women invisible to the language of harassment; collusion with abusers by dismissing harassment as harmless or normalising abuse as typical male behaviour; the long-term effects of the exodus of feminist women from the church; the isolating, exploitation, and bullying of women and others; the ongoing exclusion of the LGBTQ+ community; the facilitation of abuse through purity culture and conservative evangelical teaching, often exercised through what is arguably an irresponsible use of scripture; and the enduring effects of clericalism in a culture that privileges clergy, gives them a high degree of trust whether this is deserved or not, and creates the conditions for abuse to occur.

As the global online movements #MeToo and #ChurchToo highlighted, sexual abuse is one way of keeping women out of, or subordinate in, formerly male spaces. Like other forms of sexual violence, clergy abuse is primarily motivated and facilitated by power. This dysfunctional expression of power is equally apparent in the responses of church leaders to abuse disclosures. The process is often made so difficult for women that they give up and go away. While this obstructive response to clergy abuse continues, nothing will change. Thankfully, some churches are now moving towards less defensive and more thoughtful ways of addressing the clergy abuse crisis. In many cases, this has been driven by the efforts of survivors to challenge existing policies and praxis. Recent Royal Commissions of Inquiry in Australia, the UK, and now, Aotearoa New Zealand have highlighted abuse in faith-based institutions and made it harder for churches to hide. To conclude this study, I now consider some paths the churches need to follow to address this issue.

Jacinda Thompson

In Aotearoa New Zealand, a few courageous individuals have been instrumental in publicly calling the Anglican Church to account and have contributed significantly to the vital discussion on appropriate reform and redress. Jacinda Thompson was among those who gave evidence publicly to the Royal Commission.[1]

Thompson's husband first reported the abusive behaviour of Michael van Wijk, her parish priest, in 2005, after his wife broke down and told him some details of it. She had been seeing van Wijk for bereavement counselling and spiritual guidance after the death of her baby son, and the abuse occurred in this context, as he manipulated theological concepts to justify his behaviour – inviting her to 'come to the Father' for comfort, claiming he wanted to show his 'Jesus servant heart', and that he was giving her a 'holy kiss'. At one point, van Wijk told Thompson he could see a vision of Jesus cradling her son. Thompson later became aware that clergy knew of concerns about van Wijk's behaviour with another woman at that time. After an unsatisfactory attempt to address this issue with the Diocese of Nelson, Thompson took her complaint to the police and through civil proceedings. In 2016, 11 years after first alerting the church to van Wijk's behaviour, she instigated a Title D disciplinary process, a course of action she had previously been dissuaded from by church leaders. Van Wijk was finally deposed in 2017. Two clergy involved in the poor handling of Thompson's complaint eventually became bishops, a third was a bishop at the time. In 2020, Thompson went to a Human Rights Review Tribunal, proceedings she had initiated in 2016 and decided to follow through as a means of achieving open justice when the church failed to publish the findings of their Title D process. The church agreed a settlement which included a $100,000 redress payment, a detailed public apology,[2] and an undertaking to reform the diocese's health and safety policy. At Thompson's request, she spoke at the church's annual governance meeting, General Synod/Te Hīnota Whānui, on this issue in 2020. She comments (Abuse in Care 2020b, 470):

> In my experience, the Church behaves differently in public than behind closed doors and survivors are treated better when the Church's actions can be seen by all. It appeared to me that when the media reported the arguments the Church were defending my claim with, they then had a change of heart, dropped most of them and had a renewed interest in settling.[3]

Despite the efforts of some in the church, including Thompson and Louise Deans, it is clear that the church will only improve its practice if it is held publicly to account. Additionally, it must allow itself to be advised by survivors if it is first, to prevent abuse from happening, and second, to offer a survivor-focussed and trauma-informed approach to survivors who disclose abuse. Prompted in part by Thompson's claim and initiative, by an increasing number of claims in recent years,[4] by the obvious flaws in Title D, and in anticipation of the Royal Commission, the Anglican Church in Aotearoa New Zealand has taken significant steps to revise its disciplinary canons and to begin to establish a redress process. Whether the wider New Zealand Anglican community is fully aware of this, and whether it will commit to tackling the issue of church-based abuse remains to be seen. Archbishop Philip Richardson comments:

> I think part of the problem is not having a clear discourse across the church around why [clergy misconduct] isn't acceptable. One of the biggest challenges we have is not even whether or not our complaints handling processes are robust and survivor-driven and trauma-informed, or our redress, our currently non-existent redress processes are the same. Equally important is the whole kind of educational challenge that's in front of us. We worked really hard because of the changes to the Title D legislation[5] making online boundary courses available to all of our licensed clergy, lay people, and those with PTOs,[6] and our Ministry Educator gave me some really distressing figures. A quarter of our licensed clergy didn't even bother to turn up. A third of our PTOs didn't. But, more positively, an unprecedentedly high number of our lay leaders turned up for boundaries courses. It's the clergy that have been complaining about the increased compliance requirements. It now means that all my licensed clergy and PTOs are going to get a letter from me saying 'this is a compliance issue, your license is dependent on it'. And we will offer the courses again.

The consequences of the failure of church leaders to prioritise education and training and to weed out potential abusers are tragically evident in Thompson's story. Thompson and her family left the congregation they had belonged to for four years, where she ran the crèche and assisted at Communion, while van Wijk and his family remained and received support. The loss of their church community was understandably hard for Thompson and her children. The abuse compounded the trauma of her bereavement, adversely affecting her mental health, causing her to feel suicidal and affecting her ability to work. She left the church in 2005 and returned in 2010, for some years attending sporadically and with difficulty. The church's failure to be open about van Wijk's behaviour contributed to this. She describes feeling conflicted in her faith and doubting her own judgement as a result of the abuse and the church's handling of it. Her attempts to ensure van Wijk was prevented from abusing again in his role as a priest, to call the church to account, and to attain redress have dominated 16 years of her life.

How does the church stop abuse happening?

Mark Laaser, a pastor and counsellor who was taken to court by three clients for boundary violations asks, '[c]ould anyone anywhere have seen my problem and helped prevent me doing what I did?' (Friberg and Laaser 1998, x). One obvious response to this is that people do often see the problem, but fail to act.[7]

It became evident to Thompson that the clergy who dealt with her complaint about van Wijk were already aware of concerns about his conduct with women (Abuse in Care 2020b, 441), yet their correspondence shows that they hoped to facilitate van Wijk's return to ministry (ibid. 479–480). Despite the diocese having sexual harassment guidelines in place at the time, which clearly stated that responsibility for any such boundary violations lay solely with clergy, the clergy who dealt with this matter showed an extraordinary degree of pastoral insensitivity and procedural ineptitude. The abuse was minimised as 'not really serious' and 'pretty low end, compared to what's going on overseas' (ibid. 443). Van Wijk's behaviour was likened to that of someone who shoplifts by absent-mindedly, rather than intentionally, walking out with an unpaid for item (ibid. 477). He was not deposed until the issue was forced by the Title D process instigated by Thompson in 2016.

Similarly, there was clearly a degree of collusion with McCullough's behaviour in the Christchurch Diocese (discussed in Chapter 2). It is easier to understand why this occurs when abusers are viewed in the context of an institution that emphasises forgiveness and reconciliation; where bishops are given both disciplinary power and pastoral responsibility; if we consider the collegiality of men who have trained together and progressed through the church's ranks together; and when we recognise that people are not one-dimensional and we appreciate the perceived tragedy attached to ending a bright or talented priest's ministry on the basis of a moral lapse. However, these considerations need to be viewed in the broader context of a church that continues to devalue women and women's ministry and to prioritise men at any cost.

These issues are apparent as a priest from the diocese tells me of his experience of McCullough and the lack of resolution accompanying the case:

> Rob was really well known and well respected throughout New Zealand for his liturgical work and ministry courses, which makes it even harder. He was very involved in ministry formation and the selection process for ordination.
>
> There were rumours. It was a confusing time for me because on one hand he was very supportive and very encouraging of me. Particularly pastorally, he was wonderful. So that was one side of it. But the other side – women would visit him in his office, and they'd come out, and I could see that there was something going on that was more than just normal pastoral care.
>
> So occasionally you'd see things. I remember at a ball he had his hand down the back of the dress of one of the women – that sort of thing. So, you'd see that, and you'd try and process that, and I think it was at that point I said to my girlfriend, 'watch out for this man'. And you'd hear things. At one level, you wouldn't believe what you heard and then at another level, when you started to hear it from a number of different sources, you started to realise that what was going on was quite big.
>
> It was later on at clergy conferences, that the men would say things like, 'the feminists have ganged up against him'. It came up in clergy conferences for a number of years. When it really blew up, I remember going to the dean and saying, 'what's happening with Rob McCullough?' and he said, 'you can ask me, but I can't tell you'. And I said, 'ok', and I left it. And then at the conference, he was trying to address it, and there were groups of men saying 'oh, they're all feminists and they're just out to get him'. And I can remember saying 'no', because I'd known a few women he'd been involved with – not all of them were priests – and I said, 'this has happened', and they said, 'don't be silly'. They'd try and minimise it. And there were some women clergy who were quite anti the women as well. They'd say to the other women clergy, 'for goodness' sake, grow up and pull your heads in'.
>
> I remember one session that went on and on, so I went up to the bishop afterwards and I said, 'look this belongs with the police, why can't we just take it to the police?' And he said, 'the women

don't want it'. It was a shutting down of the legal, state processes that are nothing to do with the church. I can remember sitting there getting more and more frustrated thinking, 'this has legal ramifications, what's happened here?' I was just the young, pimply curate and he shut me down and said, 'no, the women don't want to do that'. So, we were trying as a church to address something that we had no protocols around, but we weren't prepared to use the law of the land.

I think for me the painful thing is that at clergy conferences – it often comes up obliquely – the diocese seems to oscillate between trying to expunge the whole memory of it and move on, or to put it in the past, without any acknowledgement at all of Rob having done anything good. So, one side is, 'nothing happened, just get over it' and the other side is, 'something terrible happened, so we're going to expunge the memory and with that any good that Rob ever did, including his contribution to the prayer book'.[8] I think, on reflection, a more mature position is to say well actually he did have some good points. I think to demonise someone is as bad as ignoring the other side.

The church should probably have prosecuted, but I don't think at the time that they could have coped with it. It would have taken it outside the church and possibly even more women would have come forward and had some acknowledgement and maybe some healing. It would have objectivised it. The women, including those who supported them, were labelled as witches who were just 'after him'.

He used his power over the women who were in training, or who wanted to be ordained. He used that power to get them to have an affair with him. They didn't really realise at the time what was going on. I think because there wasn't a network of people talking to each other until later, they thought they were on their own. They almost thought that's what they were meant to do, that it was part of the process. I think some of them felt genuine affection towards him, and they thought he did for them. He had this glamour, and he could be charming. So, I think they were sucked into that. It affected their lives and their ministries.

At that time, and I think still, to be a clergywoman was hard – they didn't get good jobs. They'd get parishes that were falling to bits or were part time. They had to struggle to get a job and not necessarily be accepted by parishioners. For example, I remember that in our parish we had a woman curate at the time and people would cross the church to not take Communion from her. We were still trying to establish women's ministry as being authentic and there was a lot of negativity. So, women didn't want to say, 'this is what happened', because that made them even more vulnerable and unemployable. Some of them went on to have good ministries, others were adversely affected because they spoke out. Some of them, it put them right off. There's a variety of responses.

Since the Royal Commission, I know the bishop is very keen to have some public acknowledgement of what the women went through. I think for a lot of people who have come in since, they're a bit mystified about it because they don't know any of the history and you can't actually say well, 'this is what happened', because it's very hard to measure what happened. Because it didn't go to court, there's no official story, so you can't say to people who've come into the diocese since then, 'look, this is what happened'.

When Louise's book came out [Deans 2001], that caused a lot of ruckus again. I guess having the Royal Commission has brought it all up again.

Deans made a legitimate decision to take this matter to the Royal Commission. The reality is that unless such situations are managed well by the church in the first instance, it is highly likely they will keep coming up. Many victims do not disclose their abuse for decades and the Commission is anticipating further historic revelations. The repercussions are long-lasting. Clearly McCullough's behaviour was supported by a climate of negativity towards women in ministry, and by patriarchal attitudes to sex, gender, and power. These persist. It is only when we fully address these issues, that abuse will stop. Equally, it is naive to think that the church has changed sufficiently that clergy abuse is now consigned to the past. It is not and there is still significant room for improvement in the way disclosures are managed. Because of the secrecy enforced in such cases when formal complaints are made, the church is still able to hide its failings in this area.

Clergy like van Wijk, McCullough, 'Jim', Bishop Peter Ball, and the British priest I spoke of in Chapter 2 easily manipulate situations to their advantage and sway opinion in their favour. Well-meaning colleagues and parishioners are often as fooled as the unsuspecting women who become victim to their exploitative behaviour. Some men support perpetrators as they secretly envy their apparent 'success' with women and experience a degree of vicarious satisfaction through their collusion (Rutter 1989, 71). This is why transparency is essential. In each of these cases others were aware to some extent of the behaviour and did nothing to stop it. Instead, clergy and church leaders colluded with the abusers, at least for a time, by allowing them to either continue in their roles or move to others. In these cases, as in many others, victims were blamed and left unsupported, and their efforts to disclose abuse, seek justice, and prevent harm to others were met, in some quarters, with disrespect and disregard. It is imperative that predatory clergy are removed from ministry and prosecuted where appropriate (Fortune 2013, 15–16).

Some clergy flounder professionally and pastorally in a way that is out of character, for other reasons; relationship breakdown, stress, burnout, ill health, or trauma are obvious examples. Appropriate and timely pastoral responses are crucial to prevent such situations escalating, and with adequate intervention, some can be supported to return to responsible ministry (Fortune, 2013, 15). For this to happen, it is essential that clergy and lay people feel safe to seek help. This is where the ability to have open and honest conversations about power and sexuality that are not clouded by narrow theological perspectives, thinly veiled prejudices, and a masculinist worldview is essential.

As Richardson discusses some of the changes that have occurred in the course of his ministry, he gives a different perspective on the expectation Jane outlined in Chapter 2 that young male curates would look for a wife among their congregations. This is a good example of the need for education and culture change across the church. It is not only clergy who need training. Lay people can be equally complicit in propping up clericalism and can be the first to victim-blame rather than see their beloved priest fall off his pedestal.

I was ordained at 23 but Belinda and I had known each other since we were 15, and we're still together. I was in a very secure relationship, but I was aware that other single curates going into the first parish were regarded by some of the mothers of young unmarried daughters as being good marriage possibilities, and it was accepted that you were fair game.

I remember my vicar in one parish, when I was a curate, described a former curate having what he called an 'old-fashioned affair' with a parishioner; and the sense of that was, 'well people make mistakes, and we need to forgive the mistake'. There was no sense of any understanding of the power dynamic that was at stake there. And the example of a single male curate being seen as a potential marriage option was part of that culture. So, the change in my working lifetime has been really significant.

The first time I recall, in professional development sessions, us talking about power imbalance and inappropriateness of any kind of intimate relationship, whether physical, emotional, or spiritual with a parishioner was really in the immediate post-McCullough period. It was also at around the time where women were increasingly involved in training, both as part of the training cohort and as trainers. I think of people like Susan Adams, Jean Brookes, and Heather Brunton,[9] some of those early ordained women who to my unending gratitude, would sit me down consistently as a young priest and really try to influence my thinking and my attitudes, at times being quite confrontational. I'm incredibly grateful for the robust way in which they used to call me to account.

I think part of the problem has been that we don't know how to navigate these situations and we, in the church, often have a very judgmental or very narrow take on sexuality. So, maybe it becomes too hard to look at, too scary.

Yes, it feels to me like we have spent a long time with our priorities in the wrong place, and we have spent an awful lot of time and energy and angst around attitudes and approaches to human sexuality, wrestling with each other over whether same-sex marriages could be blessed or not, at the same time as failing to really take seriously harassment and abuse in the church. We've been overly moralistic in one area, while lacking in responsibility in another.

A key thing for me is, in a way it goes back to the issue of our use of inclusive language or our use of exclusive language – and you can almost see a parallel and relation to treaty knowledge and education[10] – you cannot assume that one generation builds on the experience and the learning of the next. We need to recognise that good behaviour cannot simply be assumed. This is what I like about our Title D. I think its ministry standards are very aspirational. I mean, I don't meet all of those standards, holiness of life, for example. It is aspirational, so it's a very high bar, and if you set a high bar, you can't just leave people swinging. You really have to be attending to the educational consequences of such high bars.

I don't think that we can assume that we've learned from the past. Yes, we've got really robust selection processes in place now compared to the past, rigour around psychological testing, in this diocese anyway, before you even are allowed to enter the discernment process. But that's the minimum threshold. Our standards have to apply lifelong.

I've been very fortunate, I acknowledge that, not that I'm suggesting that marriage is easy, but I've been in a strong relationship with a person who I established a strong friendship with as a teenager, and that's been enduring for us and it's been a pivot point for me. And I am aware there have probably been moments where the importance of that relationship to me has meant that I haven't allowed myself to be exposed to other potential relationships. What I don't have a sense of, particularly before I became a bishop, is of my church tending to that with me. It was just assumed I would take responsibility. As I say, the fortunate thing for me was that I was in this kind of strong personal relationship cocoon which meant that I didn't have to face some of the things that I've seen men and women in ministry face, and therefore I find myself not able to be judgmental around other choices and decisions being made. What I can be judgmental about is that I don't think we've been attentive enough as a church, in supporting the huge challenge of maintaining respectful relationships.

I wholeheartedly agree with Richardson's assessment. Christianity is built on the teachings of Jesus who was deeply respectful to those who were marginalised, and not afraid to call out wrongdoing. Respectful relationships and accountability are foundational to resolving the issue of abuse in the church, and much else besides.

Biblical and theological responses

Churches do not prioritise sexual violence because they fail to recognise it has a theological dimension (Tombs 2017, 81). How churches think theologically about relationships and gender is crucial to how churches prevent and respond to abuse. I discussed the problematic uses of scripture and theology that sustain abuse in Chapter 3. Here I draw on two pieces of biblical and theological interpretation by David Tombs which are particularly helpful in repairing the church's response to clergy abuse.

The first is his reflection on the biblical narrative of King David (2 Samuel 15–20) who flees from Absalom, effectively leaving his concubines to be raped or killed (Tombs 2018). In this story, David, acting under the guise of leadership and with the privilege of kingship, fails his concubines by knowingly placing them at risk of violation. Next, humiliated by Absalom's abuse of the concubines, David's sexual property, David displaces his own shame by punishing, isolating, and abandoning them. This 'secondary victimisation' amplifies the stigma experienced by the abused women (Tombs 2018, 126–127).

As Tombs (p. 125) highlights, the text focusses on the story from David's perspective, ignoring the experience of the women who have been raped because David has failed in his duty of care. Tombs asks us to problematise the reading: to view it from the perspective of the ten women. It is unlikely that David has simply been reckless, we know that he is no fool. The threat from Absalom is explicit and sexual violence against the women and girls of enemy tribes and nations was an established practice then, as it is now. It is therefore reasonable to assume that David has left the women as a decoy to be violated by Absalom, while he and the rest of his household escape (pp. 129–130).

It is perhaps not too big a stretch to draw a parallel between King David in this narrative and the bishops and church leaders who have left abusive clergy in post or relocated them to other parishes to protect the reputation of the church, while blaming and shaming the victims of abuse, a form of secondary victimisation. Addressing this secondary victimisation of abuse victims is, Tombs argues, essential if churches are to support survivors and 'challenge the rape-supporting discourses that sustain such violence' (p. 127).

If the story of David's neglect and abuse of his concubines helps us to understand the role of church leaders who have thrown women and children to the wolves by failing to weed out and remove abusive clergy from their positions, and by re-victimising survivors when abuse is disclosed, there is an alternative biblical model that may prove redemptive, both for survivors and for the church as it seeks to eliminate sexual abuse within its walls.

Until recently, theological reflection on the crucifixion of Christ has tended to obscure the sexual abuse of stripping and forced nudity and to ignore the distinct possibility that Jesus experienced further sexual violence as part of the routine practice associated with that form of public humiliation, torture, and execution.[11] Yet the sexual abuse of Jesus offers a potentially liberating model for survivors and a redemptive model for the church (Figueroa and Tombs 2021). Jesus was sexually humiliated by public strippings and naked exposure on the cross (Matthew 27:28–35). He may have been further sexually assaulted by Roman soldiers, as was likely the practice during Roman crucifixions (Tombs 1999, 100–107; 2014, 160). Knowing that Jesus suffered in this way may help to reduce the shame and stigma felt so keenly by victims of abuse.

However, thus far the church has failed to incorporate the sexual abuse of Jesus during crucifixion into its theology, teaching, and iconography. Jesus' genitals are usually covered in sanitised artistic representations of the crucifixion (Reaves and Tombs 2021, 1–3). This avoidance of the abuse of Jesus is arguably linked to the closely related affects shame and disgust and represents an attempt to deflect or deny feelings of vulnerability.[12] The stigma attached to being sexually abused is such that the church has been unable to acknowledge this facet of the Saviour's experience. To recognise that Jesus was sexually abused is to place him in what is implicitly, in masculinist (hence heterosexist) cultures, a feminised and therefore shameful position; it is incongruent and intolerable in the dominant discourse that asserts the deity is male. 'Real men' do not get raped. It is to admit that men and even a male god are deeply vulnerable to violation and shame.

The control of populations via public humiliation was a central goal in execution by crucifixion. By continuing to endorse the stigma associated with sexual abuse through victim-blaming and avoiding responsibility, the church maintains itself as a masculinist system. In moving away from a defensively sanitised version of the crucifixion and acknowledging the grim reality of the cross the church may be prompted to develop a healthier and more compassionate approach to those affected by sexual abuse. As Reaves and Tombs (2021, 10) argue, acknowledging the reality of the crucifixion as involving sexual humiliation and possible further assault 'can help to expose and challenge the stigma that many in the churches mistakenly impose on survivors of abuse'.

The transformative power of speaking out

I have used the terms 'victim' and 'survivor' for expedience in this book. They are sticky terms and I find myself loathe to apply them to my own experience. Both seem to denote an ongoing, fixed, and permanent state.[13] Perhaps this is resistance to acknowledging the truth of what happened, or perhaps the events are simply distant enough in time that those terms no longer feel accurate. Certainly, the process of researching and writing this volume has helped me to move on. The bottom line is, I do not wish to be defined by the negative actions of others. These were episodes in my life that I wish had not happened and they certainly impacted adversely on the way my life has unfolded, particularly with respect to my vocation and spirituality. They are not the essence of who I am. God has remained present. My sense of vocation persists after 50 years – church or no church. To an extent it has found expression in other ways, through my research and writing and in my pastoral approach to patients and clients. However, God, it seems, keeps putting me back in the church despite my attempts to leave it behind, and in order to be here, I am compelled to make sense of my past experiences.

Commenting on openness to transformation as ethical practice, Lisa Spriggens (2018, 214) observes that '[a]llowing the people, and their stories, to change us and how we see the world and our place in it invites us into a different relationship with our self'. The Christian churches have a long and sorry history of clergy sexual misconduct. This has impacted on the lives of children, women, and men over centuries. Many churches are now seeking to address the issue of clergy abuse. Some are more committed than others. Women are still excluded from leadership in many churches globally, and many of those in same sex relationships are excluded from leadership and the public acknowledgement and blessing of their personhood and partnerships. So long as these destructive masculinist and fundamentally unchristian patterns of being church continue, clergy abuse will be with us. For those churches who are able to recognise that all God's people are created equal and are committed to women's ministry and leadership, the stories told here are an invitation to them to re-assess their understanding and practice around clergy misconduct.

Research 'changes lives' (Moschella 2008, 11). This has certainly been the case for me. Revisiting the story of my own experiences of clergy misconduct and exploring the broader contexts in which they occurred brought them more clearly into focus. In lifting my shame-filled memories out of the purely subjective realm of my personal history and locating them in the broader socio-religious discursive field that produced them, I realised that a) I was not alone and b) I was not wholly to blame. In a context where victims of clergy misconduct are too often urged to forgive their abusers, doing this research has enabled me to forgive myself.

An unexpected consequence of my research was that as people expressed interest in my work, I found myself increasingly able to discuss it frankly. My first attempts at describing my experience were with other women who had generously written or spoken about their own experiences of clergy abuse and who were equally generous in listening to some of my story. Next, I shared the proposal for this book with post-graduate research colleagues and shortly after that with the pastoral group at St John's College who had thoughtfully invited me to join their weekly online meetings during Covid lockdown. The empathy and whole-hearted support I received from these people, from others in the college community and from the clergy I spoke to, women and men from a range of cultures and religious backgrounds, helped me to move on. I have asserted elsewhere (Clough 2017, 181) that having our shame stories received with empathy helps us to overcome that shame. It is a joy to experience for myself this resolution to a journey in which shame took me, for 30 years, away from the faith community in the country of my birth.

For me, the story looks like it may well have a happy ending. A conversation with a bishop about my research on clergy abuse was met with a genuine offer of help and his declaration that the church must be accountable. That support has materialised in very practical ways, not least in support for both my academic work on shame and gender violence in the church, and my vocation and ministry.

Research of this nature, of people and communities in their socio-cultural contexts, can also be a catalyst for wider community-based and social transformation (Moschella 2008, 12). Rather than a hollow or grudgingly given apology of the type offered to some survivors of clergy abuse, my story has been met with what has thus far proved to be a genuine commitment on the part of some church leaders in Aotearoa New Zealand to addressing this fundamental sickness in the church through research and education. This is in addition to the policy changes that are already underway. It is my sincere hope that the stories in this book might inform a more compassionate and just response to victims and survivors of clergy sexual misconduct and indeed, that this work might contribute to a deeper understanding of sexual abuse and a commitment on the part of churches to strive to prevent it happening in the future.

Commenting on the UK Inquiry, Gilo, a campaigner and survivor of clergy sexual abuse suggests that the Church of England now needs to back up its apologies by real practical support for those whose lives have collapsed under the secondary victimisation delivered by the church's structure; its hierarchy, lawyers, and insurers (BBC Radio 4, 2020). This is an indictment of the way this monolithic institution has re-victimised survivors in its concerted efforts to preserve its reputation. I am profoundly grateful that I have not had a similar experience in Aotearoa New Zealand. The proactive response of church leaders on hearing the bones of my story pre-empted any need for me to actively seek redress in this province of the church. This means I have not been re-traumatised by intrusive questioning, expressions of doubt or attempts to shift blame, by unwillingness to acknowledge the flawed nature of the church, or by a protracted and stressful legal process. Sadly, as I have noted and as the stories in this book demonstrate, my experience in this regard is unusual. However, my point is that meaningful reparative action has been offered – and it is doing its job. If this is true for me, it can be true for others.

Pathways to addressing clergy abuse: what needs to happen?

In the UK, Gilo suggests that senior figures in the Church of England should consider resigning, noting that, despite being well aware of its failings in this area, the church has been slow to act. He suggests that truth and reconciliation processes between individual bishops and individual survivors would be more meaningful than what are perceived as empty apologies and advocates that mandatory reporting of all cases is built into the church's legal framework (BBC Radio 4, 2020).

In Aotearoa New Zealand, as I have noted, significant changes are currently being put in place in the Anglican Church to address clergy misconduct and establish a redress process. On the basis of her experience of seeking justice through a number of avenues, Jacinda Thompson advocates an open justice process. The church must be transparent and publicly accountable in its response to abuse. In addition, there needs to be a commitment to education and training, and to theological and ecclesiastical revision and renewal. The Anglican Church prides itself on being a 'broad' church; a church which tolerates a range of theological and ecclesiastical perspectives and expressions. Arguably, it tolerates some things it should not, including overt discrimination and abuse, and some very rusty language and biblical hermeneutics. The church needs to draw a line under those practices that are unjust, exploitative, and oppressive.

Addressing the observations of New Zealanders who participated in the Wilberforce Foundation's survey into faith and belief in New Zealand (McCrindle 2018) would be one place to start. Listening intently to the feedback and advice of survivors of clergy sexual misconduct is another. It is time to lift the veil of secrecy that surrounds wrongdoing in the church, which is often maintained under the guise of 'confidentiality', and to put a stop to the squeamishness that the church has around talking honestly about sex while being far too preoccupied with policing it in unhealthy and counterproductive ways.

This book has not focussed on the practical aspects of safeguarding so much as on the conditions that allow abuse to flourish. I would, however, like to briefly highlight some of the strategies that I believe churches would do well to put in place.

Darryl Stephens (2013, 27–29) outlines five pragmatic questions to help safeguard against professional misconduct, which I have summarised here:

1   How would others view my actions?
2   Are my actions in the best interest of the congregant or am I simply meeting my own needs?
3   What type of professional support am I offering? Sexual intimacy is not a function of ministry.

4 Does my behaviour hold up? What would my colleagues/supervisor think of it?
5 Will anyone suffer from my actions?

In addition to this, Stephens offers a framework for clergy to consider when their actions may be slipping towards misconduct.

1 Might my actions be misunderstood?
2 Does my motivation stem from my own self-importance or need to be needed?
3 Does the congregant exhibit signs of emotional dependency or am I becoming dependent on this contact with them?
4 Am I normalising unsafe behaviour? Might my actions make the congregant vulnerable to sexual predators in the future.
5 Am I deluding myself that this relationship is special, and the rules don't apply?

These safeguards are not self-evident and should be clearly taught both within ordination and post-ordination training programmes and in congregations and other church groups. Even this small amount of knowledge might have saved me a lot of distress.

Emily Colgan is one of a group of theologians in Aotearoa New Zealand who have devised an education programme on sexual abuse which is being taken up by the Catholic Church and seminaries in New Zealand.[14] I asked her what needs to happen.

I don't think there's a silver bullet, it requires an entire cultural paradigm shift. So many things need to change on a whole lot of different levels. I'm worried that the church thinks that if it gets its policies sorted, the problem will go away. But it's not a policy problem, that's the easy bit. It's the education, the bits that are intangible, that you can't just get lawyers to sort out. That has to happen at the grassroots. I don't know how much awareness of that need there is, and how much awareness of the urgency to address that need there is.

Colgan's description of the programme helpfully underlines the factors that need to be considered by churches if they are to effectively respond to sexual harassment and abuse.

Our workshop is not a silver bullet either, but I think it gives people space to recognise the issue of sexual abuse, to recognise how pervasive it is, to start being aware and attentive to the ways, conscious and unconscious, we provide a context in which abuse and violence can flourish.

It's not just a response that says, 'let's get our policies right' or 'what is the healthiest, best practice response to people who make disclosures?' It goes beyond that. The workshop starts off by naming some of the issues, looking at some of the statistics in New Zealand from the Department of Justice. It says, 'these are the statistics we're dealing with in our society, chances are these are going to be reflected at some level in your congregations. So, whether you know about violence and abuse which is happening in your congregations or not, chances are that it's there'. And we also start at that point saying, these are some of the myths, the rape myths, the purity myths, that exist in secular society, which encourage these statistics, and which enable the rates of sexual violence to be so high and the rates of conviction for sexual offending to be so low. We talk about some of those secular myths, how the media reports sexual violence and so on, and then we look at how this is articulated in Christian contexts, which is where we talk about purity culture.

Then we do some work around first responders. Signs to look for when people come and talk to you, signs of abuse in children and in adults, some of the nuances of historical abuse in comparison to more recent abuse. We do some work on what are the appropriate responses, the check list of things that you really need to tick off before that victim/survivor leaves your space. About affirming them in their experience, believing them, making sure they are safe. And then we explore some longer-term pastoral responses, making sure that the *responder* is ok after that encounter, because there can be secondary trauma as well.

So, there are the immediate pastoral and practical responses, and then we look at some of the things that churches do or say, that can be either a help or a hindrance to contexts where violence and abuse can flourish. We look at biblical texts which discuss sexual violence. Rather than just skip over them or pretend they're not there, we talk about them and say, 'how do we deal with these texts in our congregations, in preaching, in bible studies? How do we not ignore or excuse them? How do we use them as a springboard to meaningful conversations where people have the opportunity to discuss and share, and come forward with their own experiences?' I often work in contexts where discussion around sexual violence is culturally and theologically taboo. In these contexts, the Bible can function as a safe point of entry into difficult conversations about sexual violence: if the Bible talks about it, so can we. We take a similar approach with theologies. We interrogate the theological ideas and language that we use; concepts like forgiveness and reconciliation, and how those might potentially be problematic for people who are being encouraged to 'forgive and forget' as a response to sexual violence. We work with the issue of sexual violence from a number of angles to make sure people respond appropriately at an immediate pastoral and practical level, but also are cognisant of those intangible, more symbolic actions, behaviours, and words that might inadvertently contribute to a situation where violence is able to flourish, and perpetrators are able to justify and get away with violent and abusive behaviour.

Having reformed its disciplinary process and begun to consider a mechanism for redress, I hope that the Anglican Church in Aotearoa New Zealand will now take advantage of the expertise offered in this programme. It must work not only to respond well to disclosures of abuse, and to discipline clergy who offend, but first and foremost to prevent sexual abuse within its walls. It will only achieve this by educating all its members: all ages, all genders, all ranks, and by dramatically reforming its theologies and its language.

Fundamentally, I believe that education and informed, respectful discussion in theological education, ministry training, church congregations and public forums are essential if things are truly to change. Attention must return to the language used in liturgy and theology. Additionally, there is a huge role for public theologians to continue to explore and challenge the conservative, masculinist theological models that disempower some individuals and communities while shoring up power for others. This is not the way of the gospel.

Churches, including the Anglican Church in Aotearoa, New Zealand, and Polynesia, which prides itself on leading the way on matters of social justice and gender, must recognise that there is a long way to go. Women are still under-represented in governance and leadership roles in the Anglican Church in this province, and indigenous women particularly are disadvantaged by gender-based violence and lack of resources. Many of them work excessive hours for little or no remuneration. In Aotearoa New Zealand, Tikanga Māori has 3% of the resources (Abuse in Care 2021c, 468) and this impacts particularly on women clergy, with few in stipendiary positions.

The small size of the church in the province of Aotearoa, New Zealand, and Polynesia makes it difficult for women to speak openly about their experiences without being recognised. This volume has not done justice to Māori women, who are disproportionately affected by sexual violence (Pihama et al. 2016).[15] I hope to rectify this in further work. In the Diocese of Polynesia, gender-based violence – some perpetrated by clergy – and poverty are among the main issues affecting women, including clergy. Sixty-four percent of women between the ages of 15–49 in Fiji, for instance, have experienced sexual or physical intimate partner violence, with churches recognising this as a significant issue (Taonga News 2017), but often failing to speak out against it, and against the misuse of scripture that is used to justify it. Biblical interpretations of male headship, power inequality in 'families, churches and societies', and men regarding women as possessions are cited as among the main reasons for the high level of gender-based violence in the pacific (Weavers 2006).[16]

In the UK, theologian Nicola Slee (2015) locates her analysis of the gendered church in the context of theologies of multiple perspectives, including black, interfaith, disability, post-colonial, and queer theologies, alerting the church to the imperative to engage with these. Women's ordination to priesthood and episcopacy, is, she says, 'only the start' of gender equality. Much remains to be done to transform the life of a church that is far more complex than it was before women were ordained. Relief that the ordination of women is now normative sits hand in hand with grief at the subsequent invisibility of lay women, and the loss of the radical, creative energy and solidarity of the 1970s and 1980s as many women clergy, possibly out of necessity, distance themselves from a critique of the hierarchy they now operate within. The cost of priesthood has been high for many women, including those marginalised by it. In the UK, Revd Eve Pitts, the first black woman to become a vicar in the Church of England, was told to resign in 1997 by the then Bishop of Birmingham, when she preached in response to the racist and sexist behaviour she encountered from colleagues in the church (Andrews 2021). There is no data available on the proportion of women clergy who are BAME (WATCH 2021). More women clergy than men are in self-supporting, rather than paid roles in the Church of England, with women in over a third of stipendiary parish posts in only eight out of 42 dioceses. Women are underrepresented in senior positions (ibid.).

Slee's analysis of the contracting Church of England, with its current conservative and largely evangelical middle ground certainly has application to concerns expressed by ordained and lay members of the Anglican Church in Aotearoa New Zealand, where I believe contextual (including feminist, queer, and post-colonial) and indigenous theologies and models of ministry to be the way forward. The contemporary church is a difficult environment to be visionary in and currently it appears that if one is to advance in terms of leadership, one must toe the line. Slee's call to bishops in the Church of England is to listen to those who feel disenfranchised and to engage with the prophetic and inclusive message of feminist and other liberation theologies. Emphasising that the body of Christ is incomplete without its laity, she urges lay people to be confident in their calling and to challenge those clergy who appear to be forgetting their primary vocation as disciples of Christ.

Greater transparency and a more extensive role for women in both ordained ministry and lay leadership positions were proposed by the Australian Royal Commission as a means of addressing the clericalism that enables abuse in the church.[17] Finnish theologian Kati Niemelä (2011) suggests that women clergy are important agents of change in the church and that they are more inclined to focus on justice and pastoral issues than men. They need to be allowed and encouraged to do so. Equally, liberation from binary gender constructs and heteronormative sexuality as determining models for Christian relational ethics are essential if transformation is truly to take place. Arguably, a radical revisioning of the church and the delegitimising of patriarchal theology and ecclesiology suggested by Ruether as early as 1985 are still necessary to put an end to clergy sexual misconduct and the violation of women's vocations to leadership and ministry in the church.

It's a system thing

Much has been made, in church responses to abuse, of reconciliation and forgiveness. As key tenets of Christian teaching, these have frequently been manipulated and misused to pressure victims to 'let it go' and to let abusers off the hook. A fresh understanding of these concepts emerged in the Anglican Church's redress hearings at the Royal Commission, where the point was (rightly) laboured by Archbishops Richardson and Tamihere: reconciliation cannot happen without justice and redress. Forgiveness is the prerogative of survivors. It is theirs to give freely, or not at all, as they see fit. To force forgiveness is a form of spiritual abuse. The only appropriate response of perpetrators is genuine remorse accompanied by an authentic commitment to change.

Much was said during the redress hearings by the Anglican bishops that demonstrated the church's leadership is committed to transparency, to proactive, preventative action, and to a survivor-focused and trauma-informed process. However, there was some reluctance to recognise clergy abuse as a structural or systemic issue and this is concerning. In his concluding remarks, Archbishop Donald Tamihere (Abuse in Care 2001c, 460) rejected a suggestion that the culture of the Anglican Church in Aotearoa New Zealand facilitates abuse, attributing it instead to 'predatory' individuals who have taken advantage of a few 'blind spots' in the church's efforts to keep people safe. This is a common misperception. I hope that this volume has demonstrated that, as Thomas Doyle (Abuse in Care 2021b, 8:6) emphasised to the Commission with reference to the Catholic Church, 'the essential causes are systemic in nature' and are 'deeply embedded in the ecclesiastical system upon which the church is built'. Success of this and other investigations, Doyle asserts (pp. 21–22:52), will lie not in the 'creation of more administrative ventures' but in the exposure and recognition of the 'toxic beliefs and arrogant and narcissistic attitudes' that continue to plague faith-based institutions.

Clergy abuse is not the responsibility of a few 'bad apples', but of the whole church – especially its leadership who, arguably, have a particular responsibility to initiate the linguistic, theological, and structural changes needed to sort it out. I refer again to Zimbardo's (2008) work on the problem of evil. The seven factors he identifies are mindlessly taking the first small step, dehumanisation of others, de-individuation of self (the anonymity conferred by wearing a uniform or adopting the mantle of an organisation, for example), diffusion of personal responsibility, blind obedience to authority, uncritical conformity to group norms, and passive tolerance of evil through inaction or indifference. We must continually take a systems approach to abuse. We must ask the fundamental questions: 'what is the situation?' and, 'where does the power lie in the system?' (ibid.). Until those with power use their authority to influence deep theological and structural change, abuse will continue. Discourse produces culture and cultural change starts with language. Church leaders need to mandate the use of language that is inclusive of all, and theologies that are respectful of all.

Conclusion

This volume has set out too many stories of abuse in the church. It has highlighted some common themes in women's experiences and in the patterns followed by abusers and by the church in its response to abuse disclosures. It has foregrounded the discursive and structural foundations that enable rape culture and facilitate abuse by church leaders and others. Clearly the church still needs a massive shakeup in terms of its gendered theological and liturgical language, fair representation in leadership and decision-making, its understanding and teaching on human sexuality, relationships, and equality, and in developing a basic, core respect for all people. Until this happens, abuse of all kinds will continue.

With continued prompting and advice from survivors, the exposure of abuse via #MeToo and #ChurchToo, and the impetus accompanying the various Royal Commissions and other investigations, it is to be hoped that the global churches are finally willing to engage with survivor-focussed and trauma-informed models of safeguarding and redress, and to prioritise the safety of the community over clerical privilege.

Notes

1 See Abuse in Care (2020b).
2 See https://www.nativity.org.nz/bishops-apology.html [accessed 31.5.2021].
3 Survivor and law professor, Julie Macfarlane (2021, 186) had a similar experience in the UK.
4 Waikato and Taranaki Anglicans (2021).
5 'Title D of Standards', the disciplinary canons of the Anglican Church in Aotearoa New Zealand and Polynesia, revised in 2020.
6 'Permission to officiate'.
7 See Rutter (1989, 9–13, 70–74) for the reasons that men collude with colleagues who violate boundaries.
8 The church has recently published a revised edition of *A New Zealand Prayer Book/He Karakia Mihinare o Aotearoa* (2020), which retains a 1989 introduction by McCullough, and prayers by James K. Baxter, a renowned New Zealand poet who is now known to have raped his wife (Roy 2019).
9 Brookes and Brunton were among the first women to be priested in New Zealand in 1977. Adams' work is referred to in Chapter 3.
10 Te Tiriti o Waitangi/The Treaty of Waitangi.
11 The sexual abuse of Jesus was first foregrounded by Tombs (1999).
12 See Clough (2017, Chapter 6) for a discussion of shame, disgust, and vulnerability.
13 See Fortune (1999, x) on the differing preferences of women for these terms, and a third – *thrivers*.
14 This programme has been devised by Emily Colgan (Trinity Methodist College), Caroline Blyth (University of Auckland), Lisa Spriggens (Laidlaw College), Rocio Figueroa (Te Kupenga Catholic Theological College), and David Tombs (University of Otago).
15 Family violence and sexual violence were rare in Māori society before colonisation (Pihama et al. 2016, 7).
16 See Lomaloma (2018) for a discussion of gender-based violence and the church's approach to it, in the Pacific.
17 See 'Anglican Church' at https://www.childabuseroyalcommission.gov.au/religious-institutions [accessed 31.5.2021].

References

Abuse in Care Royal Commission of Inquiry, 2018. 'Terms of Reference' [online] https://www.abuseincare.org.nz/library/v/3/terms-of-reference [accessed 4.5.2021].

———, 2020a. 'Statement of Louise Deans for Faith-based Redress Hearing',

———, 2020a(i). 'Transcript of Louise Deans for Faith-based Redress Hearing' [online] https://www.abuseincare.org.nz/library/v/183/statement-of-louise-deans-for-faith-based-redress-hearing [accessed 31.5.2021].

———, 2020b. 'Transcript of Jacinda Thompson for Faith-based Redress Hearing' [online] https://www.abuseincare.org.nz/library/v/177/statement-of-jacinda-thompson-for-the-faith-based-redress-hearing [accessed 28.5.2021].

———, 2021a. 'Peter Carrell Statement for Faith-based Redress Hearing',

———, 2021a(i). 'Peter Carrell Supplementary Statement for Faith-based Redress Hearing',

———, 2021a(ii). 'Transcript of Bishop Peter Carrell at Faith-based Hearing on 18 March' [online] https://www.abuseincare.org.nz/library/v/215/statement-of-bishop-carrell-for-faith-based-redress-hearing [accessed 31.5.2021].

———, 2021b. 'Submission of Thomas Patrick Doyle', 9 March [online] https://www.abuseincare.org.nz/library/v/219/statement-of-reverend-dr-thomas-p-doyle-for-the-faith-based-redress-hearing [accessed 9.5.2021].

———, 2021c. 'Transcript of Primates Faith-based Redress Hearing' [online] https://www.abuseincare.org.nz/library/v/217/statement-of-archbishop-tamihere-archbishop-fereimi-cama-and-archbishop-richardson-the-primates [accessed 26.5.2021].

Adams, Susan, 1988. 'I Am Staying'. *Accent* 3:1, 20.

———, 2015. 'Struggle and Hope, or Struggling and Hoping Still!' in Jenny Chalmers and Erice Fairbrother (eds) *Vashti's Banquet: Voices from Her Feast*. Auckland: Council for Anglican Women's Studies. 24–37.

Allan, Patricia, 1996. 'The Place of Women in the Central Administration of the Church' and 'Mopping Up' in Louise Deans (ed) *Women of Spirit*. Templeton, NZ: Hilton Press. 32–36, 62–77.

———, 2018. 'Telling our Story: Celebrating the 40th Anniversary of the Ordination to the Priesthood of Anglican Women of the Church in

Aotearoa, New Zealand and Polynesia'. *AWSC Newsletter* 8:1, 3 [online] https://www.anglican.org.nz/Women [accessed 6.5.2021].

Alvear, Rocío Figueroa and David Tombs, 2019. 'Lived Religion and the Traumatic Impact of Sexual Abuse: The Sodalicio Case in Peru' in RR Ganzevoort and S Sremac (eds) *Trauma and Lived Religion: Transcending the Ordinary*, https://doi.org/10.1007/978-3-319-91872-3_8. London: Palgrave MacMillan. 155–176.

Andrews, Becca, 2018. 'As a Teen, Emily Joy Was Abused by a Church Youth Leader. Now She's Leading a Movement to Change Evangelical America'. *Mother Jones*, May 25 [online] https://www.motherjones.com/crime-justice/2018/05/evangelical-church-metoo-movement-abuse/ [accessed 14.4.2020].

Andrews, Kehinde, 2021. 'Eve Pitts, the Church of England's First Black Female Vicar – and One of its Fiercest Critics'. *The Guardian*, 27 May [online] https://www.theguardian.com/society/2021/may/27/eve-pitts-church-of-england-first-black-female-vicar-fiercest-critics?fbclid=IwAR0 SVzWzxMmGdNbbWxqPqSVe1R60dRDpEdjm19vl8kxQtsINGfLQiAQ RPf4 [accessed 29.5.2021].

Anglican Church in Aotearoa, New Zealand and Polynesia, 2020. *A New Zealand Prayer Book/He Karakia Mihinare o Aotearoa*. Auckland: ACANZP.

Baird, Julia, and Hayley Gleeson, 2018. 'Submit to your Husbands: Women Told to Endure Domestic Violence in the Name of God'. *ABC News*, 22 October [online] https://www.abc.net.au/news/2017-07-18/domestic-violence-church-submit-to-husbands/8652028?nw=0 [accessed 19.5.2021].

Barnett, Jenna, 2019. 'Let There Be Light'. *Sojourners Magazine*, July [online] https://sojo.net/magazine/july-2019/church-sexual-abuse-hidden-light-hankel [accessed 14.4.2020].

Batchelor, Valli Boobal (ed) 2013. 'Editor's Introduction' in *When Pastors Prey: Overcoming Clergy Sexual Abuse of Women*. Geneva: WCC Publications. xv–xix.

BBC News, 2017. 'Ex-archbishop Lord Carey Resigns after Child Abuse Review'. 26 June [online] https://www.bbc.com/news/uk-england-kent-40407464 [accessed 12.8.2020].

———, 2020. 'George Carey: Former Archbishop Suspended over Abuse Inquiry'. 18 June [online] https://www.bbc.com/news/uk-england-dorset-53086234 [accessed 12.8.2020].

BBC Radio 4, 2020. *PM,* 6 October [online] https://www.bbc.co.uk/sounds/play/m000n5yr [accessed 7.10.2020].

Benton, Kerry William Kim, 2013. *Emotionality in Same-sex Attracted Men's Sexual Scripting: Four Expatriate Men in Burma Tell Their Stories.* PhD Thesis. Deakin University.

Berglund, Taylor, 2020. 'This Isn't Funny: How Should the Body of Christ Respond When Abuse Happens in the Church?' *Charisma Digital*, March [online] https://issuu.com/charismamediaproduction/docs/cm0320digital_dig [accessed 26.5.2021].

Blyth, Caroline, 2021. *Rape Culture, Purity Culture, and Coercive Control in Teen Girl Bibles*. Abingdon: Routledge.

Blyth, Caroline, Emily Colgan, and Katie B Edwards (eds) 2018. *Rape Culture, Gender Violence and Religion: Biblical Perspectives*. Cham: Palgrave MacMillan.

Booth, Pat, Marilyn Simkin, Judith Dale, and Trish McBride, 2001. 'Exit ExAlt – Expulsion or Exodus?' *Vashti's Voices* 2:8, 18–23.

Burke, Kelly, 2020. 'Sydney Anglican Priest Forced to Resign Because His Marriage Broke Down'. *The Guardian*, 14 November [online] https://www.theguardian.com/world/2020/nov/14/sydney-anglican-priest-forced-to-resign-because-his-marriage-broke-down [accessed 19.2.2021].

CathNews New Zealand, 2020. 'Church Must Tackle Spiritual Abuse'. 28 September [online] https://cathnews.co.nz/2020/09/28/spiritual-abuse/ [accessed 1.5.2021].

Clohessy, David, 2018. 'It's Time For #MeToo in the Catholic Church'. *The Guardian*, 16 August [online] https://www.theguardian.com/commentisfree/2018/aug/16/me-too-catholic-church-predator-priests-abuse [accessed 21.4.2020].

Clough, Miryam, 2017. *Shame, the Church and the Regulation of Female Sexuality*. Abingdon and New York: Routledge.

CNA Catholic News Agency, 2017. 'Peruvian Prosecutor Requests Jail for Sodalitium Founder'. 13 December [online] https://www.catholicnewsagency.com/news/37381/peruvian-prosecutor-requests-jail-for-sodalitium-founder [accessed 5.10.2021].

Collins, Natalie, 2019. 'Unstoried: Men's Abuse of Women and Girls' in Janet Fife and Gilo (eds) *Letters to a Broken Church*. London: Ekklesia. 16–20.

Commonwealth of Australia, 2017. 'Final Report, Religious Institutions: Summary'. *Royal Commission into Institutional Responses to Child Sexual Abuse* [online] https://www.childabuseroyalcommission.gov.au/sites/default/files/file-list/unredacted-volume-16-religious-institutions-book-1.pdf [accessed 4.4.2021].

Cooper-White, Pamela, 2013. 'Clergy Sexual Abuse of Adults' in Valli Boobal Batchelor (ed) *When Pastors Prey: Overcoming Clergy Sexual Abuse of Women*. Geneva: WCC Publications. 58–81.

Crary, David, 2021. 'Growing Number of Southern Baptist Women Question Roles'. *ABC News*, 25 March [online] https://abcnews.go.com/US/wireStory/doubts-southern-baptists-limits-womens-roles-76651536 [accessed 30.5.2021].

Crawford, Janet, 1997. 'Vashti's Beginnings'. *Vashti's Voices* 2:1, 3–5.

———, 2018. 'Sexist Language in 1978'. *AWSC Newsletter* 8:5, 3–4 [online] https://www.anglican.org.nz/Women [accessed 6.5.2021].

Daly, Mary, 1973. *Beyond God the Father*. Boston: Beacon Press.

Davey, Melissa, 2017. 'Bishop Greg Thompson on Being a Sexual Abuse Survivor and the Threats that Made Him Resign'. *The Guardian*, 23 March [online] https://www.theguardian.com/australia-news/2017/mar/24/

bishop-greg-thompson-on-being-a-sexual-abuse-survivor-and-the-threats-that-made-him-resign [accessed 19.5.2021].

Davis, Brian, 1995. *The Way Ahead: Anglican Change and Prospect in New Zealand*. Christchurch: Caxton Press.

Deans, Louise, 2001. *Whistleblower*. Auckland: Tandem Press.

de Pont, Karena, 2016. 'AWSC General Synod Motions'. *AWSC Newsletter* 6:4, 5–7 [online] https://www.anglican.org.nz/Women [accessed 6.5.2021].

Doyle, Thomas, 2006. 'Clericalism: Enabler of Clergy Sexual Abuse'. *Pastoral Psychology* 54:3, 189–213.

Doyle, Thomas P, Sipe AW Richard, and Patrick J Wall, 2006. *Sex, Priests and Secret Codes: The Catholic Church's 2000-year Paper Trail of Sexual Abuse*. Los Angeles: Volt Press.

Durà-Vilà, G, R Littlewood, and G Leavey, 2013. 'Integration of Sexual Trauma in a Religious Narrative: Transformation, Resolution and Growth among Contemplative Nuns'. *Transcultural Psychiatry*, 50:1, 21–46. https://doi.org/10.1177/1363461512467769.

Ellis, C, T Adams, and A Bochner, 2011. 'Autoethnography: An Overview'. *Forum Qualitative Sozialforschung / Forum: Qualitative Social Research* 12:1 [online] http://www.qualitative-research.net/index.php/fqs/article/view/1589/3095 [accessed 22.3.19].

Everhart, Ruth, 2020. *The #MeToo Reckoning: Facing the Church's Complicity in Sexual Abuse and Misconduct*. Illinois: InterVarsity Press.

Exposed: The Church's Darkest Secret, 2020. BBC. On air January 13 and 14, 2020.

Fife, Janet, and Gilo (eds) 2019. *Letters to a Broken Church*. London: Ekklesia.

Figueroa, Rocío, and David Tombs, 2021. 'Seeing His Innocence, I See My Innocence' in Jayme R Reaves, David Tombs, and Rocío Figueroa (eds) *When Did We See You Naked? Jesus as a Victim of Sexual Abuse*. London: SCM Press. 287–312.

Fletcher, Megan Alyssa, 2018. 'We to Me: An Autoethnographic Discovery of Self, In and Out of Domestic Abuse'. *Women's Studies in Communication* 41:1, 42–59, DOI: 10.1080/07491409.2017.1423526.

Fortune, Marie M, 1999. 'Foreword' in Nancy Werking Poling (ed) *Victim to Survivor: Women Recovering from Clergy Sexual Abuse*. Cleveland, Ohio: United Church Press. ix–xvi.

———, 2013. 'Sexual Abuse by Religious Leaders' in Valli Boobal Batchelor (ed) *When Pastors Prey: Overcoming Clergy Sexual Abuse of Women*. Geneva: WCC Publications. 14–21.

Friberg, Nils C, and Laaser, Mark R, 1998. *Before The Fall: Preventing Pastoral Sexual Abuse*. Collegeville, Minnesota: The Liturgical Press.

Garland, Diana, 2013. 'Don't Call it an Affair: Understanding and Preventing Clergy Sexual Misconduct with Adults' in Claire M Renzetti and Sandra Yocum (eds) *Clergy Sexual Abuse: Social Science Perspectives*. Boston: Northeastern University Press. 118–143.

Garland Diana, and Christen Argueta, 2010. 'How Clergy Sexual Misconduct Happens: A Qualitative Study of First-Hand Accounts'. *Social Work and Christianity*, 37: 1–27.

Gillett, Rachel, 2017. 'Sexual Harassment Isn't an Industry, Workplace, or Company Issue – In Fact, It Affects Nearly Everyone'. *Business Insider*, November 10 [online] https://www.businessinsider.com.au/sexual-harassment-affects-nearly-everyone-2017-11?r=US&IR=T [accessed 31.3.2021].

Gooder, Paula, 2015. 'On Getting Here From There: Reflections on the Journey to the Consecration of Women as Bishops within the Church of England' in Jenny Chalmers and Erice Fairbrother (eds) *Vashti's Banquet: Voices from Her Feast*. Auckland: Council for Anglican Women's Studies. 77–101.

Grace, Sonja, 1996. *Garlands from Ashes: Healing from Clergy Sexual Abuse*. Wanganui: The Grace-Watson Press.

Guy, Laurie, 2011. *Shaping Godzone: Public Issues and Church Voices in New Zealand 1840–2000*. Wellington: Victoria University Press.

Harper, Rosie, and Alan Wilson, 2019. *To Heal and Not to Hurt: A Fresh Approach to Safeguarding in Church*. London: Darton, Longman and Todd Ltd.

Henley, Jon, 2010. 'How the Boston Globe Exposed the Abuse Scandal that Rocked the Catholic Church'. *The Guardian*, 21 April [online] https://www.theguardian.com/world/2010/apr/21/boston-globe-abuse-scandal-catholic [accessed 4.4.2021].

Hopkins, Nancy Myer (ed) 1993. *Clergy Sexual Misconduct: A Systems Perspective*. Washington: The Alban Institute.

House of Bishops, 2019. 'Civil Partnerships – For Same Sex and Opposite Sex Couples. A Pastoral Statement from the House of Bishops of the Church of England' [online] https://www.churchofengland.org/sites/default/files/2020-01/Civil%20Partnerships%20-%20Pastoral%20Guidance%202019%20%282%29.pdf [accessed 10.5.2020].

Independent inquiry Child Sexual Abuse, 2018. 'First Witness Statement of Lord Rowan Douglas Williams in the "Anglican Church" Investigation'. 25 January [online] https://www.iicsa.org.uk/key-documents/6289/view/ACE026001.pdf [accessed 4.4.2021].

———, 2019a. 'Inquiry Publishes Report into the Diocese of Chichester and Peter Ball'. 9 May. Crown copyright [online] https://www.iicsa.org.uk/news/inquiry-publishes-report-diocese-chichester-and-peter-ball [accessed 31.3.2021].

———, 2019b. 'The Anglican Church. Case Studies 1: The Diocese of Chichester. 2: The Response to Allegations against Peter Ball. Investigation Report'. May. Crown copyright [online] https://www.iicsa.org.uk/key-documents/11301/view/anglican-church-case-studies-chichester-peter-ball-investigation-report-may-2019.pdf [accessed 5.10.2021].

———, 2020. 'The Anglican Church. Investigation Report'. October. Crown copyright [online] https://www.iicsa.org.uk/publications/investigation/anglican-church [accessed 4.4.2021].

Jamieson, Penny, 1997. *Living at the Edge: Sacrament and Solidarity in Leadership*. London: Mowbray.

———, 1998. *Dangerous Hands in Deep Waters – Some First Reflections on 2 Corinthians*. Speech to WATCH (Women and the Church). John Kinder Library: ANG 044/2/19.

Johnston, Kirsty, 2020. 'Sexual Harassment Victim Wins Landmark Apology from Anglican Church.' *New Zealand Herald*, 23 March [online] https://www.nzherald.co.nz/nz/sexual-harassment-victim-wins-landmark-apology-from-anglican-church/JOJTPPOMX4JRJFQSUMD7ONPCVM/ [accessed 4.4.2021].

Jordan, JV, M Walker, and LM Hartling (eds) 2004. *The Complexity of Connection: Writing from the Stone Center's Jean Baker Miller Training Institute.* New York: Guilford Press.

Jung, Patricia Beattie, and Darryl W Stephens (eds) 2013. *Professional Sexual Ethics: A Holistic Ministry Approach.* Minneapolis: Fortress Press.

Kennedy, Eugene Cullen, 2019. 'The Hierarchical Spirit That Will Not Die. Under Hierarchical Culture, Abuse Crisis Will Remain With Us.' *National Catholic Reporter*, 55:19, 5–7.

Kennedy, Margaret, 2013. 'Exploitation, Not "Affair" in Valli Boobal Batchelor (ed) *When Pastors Prey: Overcoming Clergy Sexual Abuse of Women.* Geneva: WCC Publications. 26–36.

Kleiven, Tormod, 2018. 'Sexual Misconduct in the Church: What Is it about?' *Pastoral Psychology* 67:277–289 [online] https://doi.org/10.1007/s11089-018-0807-3 [accessed 11.5.2020].

L'Arche International, 2020. 'Summary Report' [online] https://www.larche.org/documents/10181/2539004/Inquiry-Summary_Report-Final-2020_02_22-EN.pdf/6f25e92c-35fe-44e8-a80b-dd79ede4746b [accessed 13.6.2020].

Lomaloma, Sereima, 2018. 'Violence against Women – the Sin and its Prevention'. *Church Times*, 16 March [online] https://www.churchtimes.co.uk/articles/2018/16-march/features/features/violence-against-women-the-sin-and-its-prevention [accessed 31.5.2021].

Lovell-Smith, Rose, 1993. 'Wellington Christian Feminists 1977–1990' in Anne Else (ed) *Women Together: A History of Women's Organisations in New Zealand, Ngā Ropū Wāhine o te motu.* Wellington: Daphne Brasell Associates Press. 189–190.

Macfarlane, Julie, 2021. 'The Anglican Church's Sexual Abuse Defence Playbook'. *Theology*, 124:3, 182–189. doi: 10.1177/0040571X211008547.

Martin, Elizabeth, 2020. *A Theological Reflection on 'Hell on Earth' by Elizabeth Martin, in light of the MeToo Movement.* Unpublished essay.

MartinJenkins, 2020a. Economic Cost of Abuse in Care. 29 September [online] file:///C:/Users/mirya/Downloads/Economic-Cost-of-Abuse-in-Care.pdf [accessed 4.4.2021].

———, 2020b. Indicative Estimates of the Size of Cohorts and Levels of Abuse in State and Faith-Based Care 1950–2019. Final Report. Royal Commission of Inquiry into Historical Abuse in Sate Care and in the Care of Faith-Based Institutions [online] file:///C:/Users/mirya/Downloads/Size-of-cohorts-and-levels-of-abuse-in-State-and-faith-based-care%20(3).pdf [accessed 4.4.2021].

McBride, Trish, 1999. *From the Shepherd's Mouth: A Study of Sexual Abuse in the Church.* Wellington: Trish McBride.

McCrindle Research Ltd., 2018. *Faith and Belief in New Zealand.* Commissioned by The Wilberforce Foundation [online] https://2qean3bljjd-1s87812ool5ji-wpengine.netdna-ssl.com/wp-content/uploads/images/FaithBeliefNZ_Report.pdf [accessed 5.5.2020].

McKinlay, Judith, 1997. 'Women's Voices'. *Vashti's Voices* 2:1, 3–4.

Moschella, Mary Clark, 2008. *Ethnography as a Pastoral Practice: An Introduction.* Cleveland, Ohio: Pilgrim Press.

Neave, Rosemary (ed) 1990. *The Journey and the Vision: A Report on Ordained Anglican Women in the Church of the Province of New Zealand.* Auckland: The Women's Resource Centre.

———, 1991. 'Why a Women's Resource Centre?' in Rosemary Neave (ed) *No Longer Six Foot Above Contradiction.* Auckland: Women's Resource Centre, 28–30.

Niemelä, Kati, 2011. 'Female Clergy as Agents of Religious Change?' *Religions* 2, 358–371. [online] https://doi.org/10.3390/rel2030358 [accessed 20.10.2020].

Pelly, Jo, 1980. 'St John's College, Is It Worth It?' *Vashti's Voice* 9, 4–7.

Pihama, Leonie, Rihi Te Nana, Ngaropi Cameron, Cherryl Smith, John Reid, and Kim Southey, 2016. 'Māori Cultural Definitions of Sexual Violence'. *Sexual Abuse in Australia and New Zealand* 7:1 [online] https://researchcommons.waikato.ac.nz/bitstream/handle/10289/12338/Ma%C-C%84ori%20Cultural%20Definitions%20of%20Sexual%20Violence.pdf?isAllowed=y&sequence=11 [accessed 30.5.2021].

Poling, Nancy Werking (ed) 1999. *Victim to Survivor: Women Recovering from Clergy Sexual Abuse.* Ohio: United Church Press.

Porter, Muriel, 2015. 'Second Female Bishop Barbara Darling Broke Ground in Anglican Church'. *The Sydney Morning Herald.* 26 February [online] https://www.smh.com.au/national/second-female-bishop-barbara-darling-broke-ground-in-anglican-church-20150226-13p9lg.html [accessed 12.5.2021].

Quince, Jenny, 2018. '40 Years of Storytelling: A Reflection on Tikanga Maori Wahine Ordination Journey'. *AWSC Newsletter* 8:1, 3 [online] https://www.anglican.org.nz/Women [accessed 6.5.2021].

Rambo, Shelly, 2020. 'Foreword' in Karen O'Donnell and Katie Cross (eds) *Feminist Trauma Theologies.* London, SCM Press, xv–xviii.

Reaves, Jayme R, 2020. 'Reading the Whole Bible with Integrity: Identifying Context, Identity, Community, and Antisemitism in Christian Hermeneutical Practices'. *Journal for Interdisciplinary Biblical Studies* 2:1, 150–178.

Reaves, Jayme R, and David Tombs, 2021. 'Introduction: Acknowledging Jesus as a Victim of Sexual Abuse' in Jayme R Reaves, David Tombs, and Rocío Figueroa (eds) *When Did We See You Naked? Jesus as a Victim of Sexual Abuse.* London: SCM Press. 1–11.

Rees, Christina, 2019. 'Joining the Dots: Theology and Culture that Breed Clergy Abuse of Women' in Janet Fife and Gilo (eds) *Letters to a Broken Church.* London: Ekklesia. 136–142.

Richardson, Philip, 2015. 'Chalices and Gumboots: Developing Sustainable Rural Ministry' in Jenny Chalmers and Erice Fairbrother (eds) *Vashti's*

Banquet: Voices from Her Feast. Auckland: Council for Anglican Women's Studies. 185–207.

Roy, Eleanor Ainge, 2019. 'James K Baxter: Venerated Poet's Letters about Marital Rape Rock New Zealand'. *The Guardian*, 15 February [online] https://www.theguardian.com/world/2019/feb/15/james-k-baxter-venerated-poets-letters-about-marital-rock-new-zealand [accessed 6.5.2021].

Ruether, Rosemary Radford, 1985. *Women Church: Theology and Practice of Feminist Liturgical Communities*. San Francisco: Harper and Row.

Rutter, Peter, 1989. *Sex in the Forbidden Zone: when Men in Power – Therapists, Doctors, Clergy, Teachers, and Others – Betray Women's Trust*. New York: Fawcett Crest.

Schoener, Gary, 2013. 'Historical Reflections on Clergy Abuse' in Valli Boobal Batchelor (ed) *When Pastors Prey: Overcoming Clergy Sexual Abuse of Women*. Geneva: WCC Publications. 3–13.

Sherwood, Harriet, 2020. 'C of E Sex Guidance Row: Synod Member Calls Out 'deep' Hypocrisy'. *The Guardian* 4 February [online] https://www.theguardian.com/world/2020/feb/04/c-of-e-sex-guidance-row-synod-member-calls-out-deep-hypocrisy [accessed 10.5.2020].

Sipe, AW Richard, 2007. 'Introduction' in Anson Shupe (ed) *Spoils of the Kingdom. Clergy Misconduct and Religious Community*. Urbana and Chicago: University of Illinois Press. xv–xxvii.

Slee, Nicola, 2015. 'On Getting Here from There: Reflections on the Journey to the Consecration of Women as Bishops within the Church of England' in Jenny Chalmers and Erice Fairbrother (eds) *Vashti's Banquet: Voices from Her Feast*. Auckland: Council for Anglican Women's Studies. 220–240.

Spriggens, Lisa, 2018. 'Responding to Stories of Trauma' in Caroline Blyth, Emily Colgan, and Katie B Edwards (eds) *Rape Culture, Gender Violence and Religion: Christian Perspectives*. Cham: Palgrave MacMillan, 211–215.

Stephens, Darryl W, 2013. 'Fiduciary Duty and Sacred Trust' in Patricia Beattie Jung and Darryl W Stephens (eds) *Professional Sexual Ethics: A Holistic Ministry Approach*. Minneapolis: Fortress Press.

Stephenson, Anne, 2016. *Adult Sexual Abuse in Religious Institutions: Faith Seeks Understanding*. Wellington: Philip Garside Publishing Ltd.

Stiebert, Johanna, 2020. *Rape Myths, the Bible and #MeToo*. Abingdon, Oxon: Routledge.

Stuart, Frances, 1991. *Women and Church – To Leave or not to Leave – That Is the Question*. Auckland: Women's Resource Centre.

Taonga News, 2017. 'Break the Silence Sunday'. *Anglican Taonga*, 16 November [online] https://www.anglicantaonga.org.nz/news/tikanga_pasifika/silence [accessed 30.5.2021].

Tomazin, Farrah, 2018. 'Forgotten Victims of Priest Sexual Abuse. They Were Not Children, but Could They Consent?' *The Sydney Morning Herald*, December 9, 2018. https://www.smh.com.au/national/forgotten-victims-of-priest-sexual-abuse-they-were-not-children-but-could-they-consent-20181206-p50knj.html [accessed 20.10.2020].

Tombs, David, 1999. 'Crucifixion, State Terror, and Sexual Abuse'. *Union Seminary Quarterly Review* 53:1–2, 89–109.

———, 2014. 'Silent No More: Sexual Violence in Conflict as a Challenge to the Worldwide Church'. *Acta Theologica*, December, 34:2, 142–65. DOI: 10.4314/actat.v34i2.9 [accessed 15.6.2021].

———, 2017. 'Lived Religion and the Intolerance of the Cross' in R Ruard Ganzevoort and Srdjan Sremac (eds) *Lived Religion and the Politics of (In) Tolerance*. Cham: Palgrave MacMillan. 63–83.

———, 2018. 'Abandonment, Rape, and Second Abandonment: Hannah Baker in 13 Reasons Why and the Royal Concubines in 2 Samuel 15–20' in Caroline Blyth, Emily Colgan, and Katie B Edwards (eds) *Rape Culture, Gender Violence and Religion: Biblical Perspectives*. Cham: Palgrave Mac-Millan. 117–141.

Waikato and Taranaki Anglicans, 2021. *Boundaries 1: Royal Commission and New Ministry Standards Canons* [online] https://www.wtanglican.nz/site_files/19978/upload_files/Boundaries1RCandNewTitleD.1.pdf?dl=1 [accessed 29.5.2021].

Wakatama, Giselle, 2017. 'Newcastle Anglican Bishop Greg Thompson Quits After Working Hard to Deal with Abuse Issues'. *ABC News*, 16 March [online] https://www.abc.net.au/news/2017-03-16/newcastle-anglican-bishop-greg-thompson-quits/8359408 [accessed 19.5.2021].

WATCH (Women and the Church), 2021. *A Report on the Developments in Women's Ministry in 2020* [online] https://womenandthechurch.org/resources/a-report-on-the-developments-in-womens-ministry-in-2020/ [accessed 30.5.2021].

Weavers: Women in Theological Education, 2006. *The Church and Violence against Women*. Suva: Weavers/SPATS.

Wood, Margaret, 1988. *The Ordained Women of New Zealand as at July 1988*. NZ: Southern Research Unit, unpublished survey.

Zimbardo, Philip, 2008. 'The Psychology of Evil' [online] https://www.ted.com/talks/philip_zimbardo_the_psychology_of_evil?language=en [accessed 20.10.2020].

Index

Note: Page numbers followed by "n" denote endnotes.